Zen and the Art of COINTELPRO

Steve Short

Published by Defenestration Press, 2024.

While every precaution has been taken in the preparation of this book, the publisher assumes no responsibility for errors or omissions, or for damages resulting from the use of the information contained herein.

ZEN AND THE ART OF COINTELPRO

First edition. October 6, 2024.

Copyright © 2024 Steve Short.

ISBN: 979-8227983190

Written by Steve Short.

Table of Contents

The Eye That Sees All 1

The Illusion of Control 10

Mindfulness Under Surveillance 18

COINTELPRO's Karmic Consequences 27

The Weaponization of Fear 36

The Zen of Subversion 44

Emptiness and the FBI Files 52

Zazen in the Shadow of Big Brother 60

Disinformation as Delusion 69

Surveillance Capitalism and the New COINTELPRO 78

The Mirror of the State 88

Compassion for the Oppressor 96

Waking Up in the Panopticon 105

Breaking the Cycle of Oppression 115

The Zen of Freedom 124

The Eye That Sees All

In the shadowy depths of the Cold War, amidst the political paranoia and ideological warfare between the United States and the Soviet Union, the U.S. government found itself increasingly concerned about threats from within. The streets of America were simmering with social unrest, movements for civil rights, and anti-war protests. In this atmosphere, the Federal Bureau of Investigation (FBI) began covert operations to monitor, disrupt, and dismantle groups and individuals it deemed subversive. This was the birth of the Counter Intelligence Program—COINTELPRO—a secretive initiative that would leave a lasting impact on American society, civil liberties, and the nation's democratic ideals.

At the heart of COINTELPRO was the notion of constant surveillance—an all-seeing eye watching over the nation's supposed enemies, whether they were activists fighting for racial equality, Native American rights, or peace. But beyond the technical tools of surveillance and infiltration, COINTELPRO also operated on a psychological level, seeking to fracture social movements from within, spread disinformation, and foster an environment of paranoia. It was a war for the mind as much as for political power. The FBI's tactics resembled an omnipresent gaze, a manifestation of what philosopher Jeremy Bentham once envisioned as the "Panopticon," a structure designed for total surveillance, where people regulate their own behavior simply because they believe they are being watched.

STEVE SHORT

The Origins of COINTELPRO

The formal creation of COINTELPRO in 1956 was a direct response to rising fears of communism infiltrating American institutions. Though the program initially targeted the Communist Party USA, it quickly expanded to include a wide array of social movements. Civil rights leaders, Black nationalists, feminist groups, anti-war activists, and even members of the American Indian Movement became ensnared in the web of FBI surveillance. The stated goal of COINTELPRO was to "protect national security, prevent violence, and maintain the existing social and political order." However, the methods employed often undermined the very democratic values the government claimed to protect.

Under the leadership of J. Edgar Hoover, the FBI's mandate to protect the country morphed into a directive to control it. Hoover was notoriously distrustful of movements that threatened the status quo, especially those advocating for Black empowerment. He labeled figures like Dr. Martin Luther King Jr. and Malcolm X as dangerous agitators, believing that their influence could destabilize the nation's social fabric. This belief fueled a campaign of relentless surveillance, harassment, and manipulation aimed at neutralizing their power.

COINTELPRO operated in secrecy for nearly two decades, its existence hidden from the American public and even many within the government. Its methods were covert and insidious: wiretaps, anonymous letters designed to sow discord within organizations, infiltrators planted to disrupt activities from the inside, and smear campaigns intended to discredit leaders. At times, these tactics resulted in fatal consequences. For instance, the FBI's surveillance of Black Panther leaders Fred Hampton and Mark Clark is widely believed to have played a role in their deaths during a police raid in 1969.

At its core, COINTELPRO was designed to neutralize dissent, to prevent change, and to preserve the power structures that had long defined American society. It was an eye that saw all, but its gaze was not benevolent—it was an eye driven by fear, suspicion, and the belief that control must be maintained at all costs.

Surveillance as a Form of Control

The power of surveillance lies not just in the act of watching, but in the knowledge that one is being watched. COINTELPRO's operations were carefully constructed to create an environment of constant uncertainty and fear within activist movements. Leaders and members never knew if their phones were tapped, if the person sitting next to them at a meeting was an informant, or if their private conversations were being recorded.

This psychological pressure was a critical component of COINTELPRO's effectiveness. The FBI recognized that by cultivating an atmosphere of suspicion, they could cause movements to self-destruct from within. One of their most notorious tactics was to send anonymous letters or fabricate documents to sow discord among leaders. In the Black Panther Party, for example, the FBI sent fake letters to party leaders, leading to infighting and mistrust. Relationships that had once been built on solidarity began to erode under the strain of paranoia, and as a result, the collective power of these movements was diminished.

In a way, COINTELPRO functioned as a kind of psychological warfare. It manipulated the mind, the emotions, and the fears of those involved in social movements. And in doing so, it exposed a fundamental truth about surveillance: its goal is not merely to gather information but to control behavior. In the world of COINTELPRO, the line between surveillance and manipulation was not just blurred—it was nonexistent.

The FBI's tactics eerily mirrored the teachings of Bentham's Panopticon, a prison design where inmates could not see the guard tower but knew that at any moment they could be watched. The uncertainty of observation would compel prisoners to regulate their own behavior. COINTELPRO took this principle and applied it to the nation's political dissidents, creating a Panopticon of the mind. The fear of being watched, of having their actions monitored and their words used against them, led many activists to self-censor or withdraw from movements altogether. It was an elegant, if brutal, form of control.

Zen and the Paradox of Awareness

In contrast to the all-seeing eye of COINTELPRO, Zen philosophy offers a different kind of gaze—one turned inward. At its heart, Zen teaches the importance of awareness, but this awareness is not about surveillance or control. Instead,

ZEN AND THE ART OF COINTELPRO

it is about mindfulness: the practice of being fully present in the moment, of observing one's thoughts, feelings, and surroundings without judgment or attachment.

Zen teaches that the mind, when untrained, can be a source of suffering. It clings to fears, anxieties, and desires, constantly seeking control over situations that are inherently uncontrollable. In this way, the untrained mind mirrors the paranoia of COINTELPRO. Just as the FBI sought to control every aspect of political dissent, the mind often seeks to control every aspect of life, even though true control is an illusion.

However, through the practice of mindfulness, Zen teaches that we can learn to observe the mind's thoughts without becoming entangled in them. This is where Zen and COINTELPRO diverge so dramatically. While COINTELPRO used surveillance as a weapon to manipulate and control, Zen teaches that true power comes not from controlling external circumstances but from cultivating internal awareness. To be truly aware is to be free from the need for control.

This concept is best illustrated in the Zen practice of Zazen, or seated meditation. In Zazen, the practitioner simply sits, paying attention to their breath and the present moment. Thoughts may arise, but the goal is not to chase them or control them—only to observe them as they pass by. Over time, this practice cultivates a sense of peace and clarity, as the practitioner begins to see the world as it is, rather than through the lens of fear or desire.

STEVE SHORT

The tension between COINTELPRO's surveillance and Zen's mindfulness lies in the very nature of awareness. COINTELPRO's gaze was an attempt to impose order, to exert control over unpredictable human behavior. But Zen's awareness is about acceptance, about seeing things as they are without the need to change or control them. Where COINTELPRO sought to manipulate, Zen seeks to liberate.

The Ethics of Surveillance

COINTELPRO's surveillance tactics raise profound ethical questions about the nature of power and control in society. Is it ever justifiable to monitor citizens without their knowledge or consent? Can the need for national security outweigh the right to privacy? And perhaps most importantly, what happens to a society when its government operates in secrecy, using tactics designed to manipulate and undermine its own citizens?

For many, the revelations about COINTELPRO that emerged in the 1970s—after the program had been officially disbanded—were shocking. The idea that the FBI, an agency ostensibly dedicated to protecting the American people, had engaged in illegal activities to subvert political movements challenged the very notion of democracy. COINTELPRO represented a betrayal of the public trust, a reminder that power, when left unchecked, can become a force for oppression rather than protection.

In Zen, ethical behavior is a cornerstone of practice. The Buddhist precepts, which include commitments to non-harm, truthfulness, and respect for others, offer a framework for

ZEN AND THE ART OF COINTELPRO

living a life in harmony with the world around us. From a Zen perspective, the actions of COINTELPRO would be seen as deeply unethical, driven by fear and attachment rather than wisdom or compassion. In Zen, the pursuit of power for its own sake is a form of delusion, a grasping after an illusion that ultimately leads to suffering.

Moreover, Zen teaches that the means by which we achieve our goals are just as important as the goals themselves. COINTELPRO may have been designed to protect national security, but the methods it employed—deception, manipulation, and surveillance—created far more harm than they prevented. From a Zen perspective, such tactics would only perpetuate suffering, both for the targets of surveillance and for those who wielded the power to control them.

Self-Surveillance and the Modern World

As the 20th century gave way to the 21st, the tools of surveillance became more sophisticated, and the dynamics of control more subtle. While COINTELPRO was a secret government program, today's surveillance is often conducted in the open, through digital technology, social media platforms, and the omnipresent eyes of smartphones and cameras. Modern society has become a panopticon of its own making, where people willingly surrender their privacy in exchange for convenience or security.

In this sense, COINTELPRO was a precursor to the world we live in today—a world where surveillance is not just a tool of the state, but a fundamental part of everyday life.

Governments, corporations, and even individuals engage in constant surveillance, whether through data collection, social media monitoring, or facial recognition technology. The all-seeing eye has become a permanent fixture in modern life.

Yet Zen offers a way to navigate this surveillance-saturated world without becoming consumed by it. Through the practice of mindfulness, individuals can cultivate an awareness that transcends the need for external control. By turning inward and developing a deep understanding of their own thoughts and feelings, people can reclaim a sense of autonomy and freedom, even in a world where privacy is increasingly compromised.

In the end, the tension between COINTELPRO's surveillance and Zen's mindfulness reflects a deeper tension between fear and acceptance. COINTELPRO was driven by a desire to control, to eliminate threats, and to preserve a particular social order. But Zen teaches that true peace and freedom come not from control, but from letting go—letting go of the need to manipulate, to fear, and to dominate.

The Eye That Sees Within

The title of this chapter, "The Eye That Sees All," refers not just to COINTELPRO's gaze, but also to the gaze of the Zen practitioner. Both forms of awareness are powerful, but they serve fundamentally different purposes. COINTELPRO's eye sought to control and subjugate, while the Zen eye seeks to understand and liberate. One is motivated by fear, the other by compassion.

ZEN AND THE ART OF COINTELPRO

The story of COINTELPRO is one of surveillance gone awry, of a government's attempt to control its people through fear and manipulation. But Zen offers an alternative vision—a vision of a world where awareness leads not to control, but to peace, understanding, and the possibility of true liberation.

The Illusion of Control

Control is one of the most powerful human desires. We seek to control our environment, our relationships, our destinies, and even ourselves. Governments, institutions, and individuals alike attempt to exert control over various aspects of life in an effort to create stability, predictability, and safety. But the paradox at the heart of this pursuit is that control itself is an illusion. The more we try to control, the more we find ourselves ensnared by the very forces we are attempting to manage.

Zen philosophy cuts to the core of this paradox. One of its fundamental teachings is the idea of impermanence—everything in life is constantly changing, and nothing remains the same. This impermanence makes control not only impossible but also a source of suffering when we try to impose it. In the Zen tradition, the realization that we cannot control the world around us leads to a profound sense of liberation. To let go of control is to embrace life as it is, free from the fear that arises from our futile attempts to dominate the uncontrollable.

In stark contrast to this philosophy stands COINTELPRO, the FBI's covert Counter Intelligence Program. COINTELPRO embodied the desire for control on a societal level. It sought to manipulate the social and political landscape of the United States, infiltrating and undermining movements that challenged the status quo. The FBI's leaders, particularly J. Edgar Hoover, believed that by monitoring, disrupting, and discrediting groups such as the Civil Rights Movement and

ZEN AND THE ART OF COINTELPRO

the Black Panther Party, they could maintain control over a nation that was undergoing radical social change. But in their obsessive quest for control, COINTELPRO became trapped in its own cycle of paranoia, fear, and overreach. The very forces it sought to suppress were, in many ways, amplified by the oppressive measures taken against them.

The Nature of Control: A Double-Edged Sword

From the perspective of Zen, the desire for control is seen as one of the primary causes of suffering. In life, we are constantly confronted with situations that we cannot fully dictate: illness, aging, death, and the behaviors of others, to name just a few. Yet, despite this inherent unpredictability, we strive to control outcomes, believing that if we could just exert enough influence, everything would unfold according to our plans.

This attachment to control becomes a prison for the mind. In Zen, it is taught that clinging to control leads to an endless cycle of anxiety and disappointment. The more we attempt to grip reality tightly, the more elusive it becomes. This teaching is exemplified in the concept of *anicca*, or impermanence, which holds that nothing in life is permanent. All things are in a constant state of flux—our thoughts, our emotions, and even the circumstances of the world around us. To believe that we can control these forces is to resist the natural flow of life, which leads to suffering.

COINTELPRO was, in many ways, a manifestation of this human tendency on a grand scale. The program represented the FBI's attempt to control the social and political dynamics of a country in the midst of profound change. In the 1960s and 1970s, the United States was grappling with movements for racial equality, gender equality, and an end to war, all of which posed challenges to the established order. Rather than accepting the inevitability of change, COINTELPRO sought to suppress it. Through surveillance, infiltration, and disinformation, the FBI aimed to neutralize perceived threats to the status quo, particularly those posed by African-American leaders, leftist activists, and other progressive forces.

The irony, of course, is that COINTELPRO's attempts to control these movements often backfired. Instead of quelling dissent, the FBI's covert actions frequently fueled the very resistance they sought to destroy. By spying on civil rights leaders like Dr. Martin Luther King Jr. and planting informants in groups like the Black Panther Party, COINTELPRO created an atmosphere of suspicion and paranoia that sometimes drove activists to even more radical positions. The more the FBI tightened its grip, the more the movements slipped through its fingers.

COINTELPRO and the Quest for Control

At the heart of COINTELPRO's strategy was a deep fear—fear of communism, fear of revolution, fear of the unknown. The FBI's obsessive need to monitor and manipulate social movements was rooted in the belief that these movements, if left unchecked, would lead to the collapse of American society as it was known. In the mind of J. Edgar Hoover, the FBI's long-time director, the rise of groups like the

ZEN AND THE ART OF COINTELPRO

Black Panthers or the Students for a Democratic Society (SDS) posed an existential threat to the country's institutions and its way of life. Hoover was determined to prevent this perceived chaos by any means necessary.

But in seeking control over these movements, COINTELPRO fell victim to the very paranoia it sought to inspire in others. The FBI's internal culture became dominated by a siege mentality, in which every activist was viewed as a potential enemy, every protest a precursor to revolution. This mindset led to increasingly extreme measures: illegal wiretaps, fake letters designed to incite conflict between activists, and even efforts to provoke violent confrontations between rival factions. In its quest for control, the FBI began to act not as a defender of democracy, but as a force of repression.

One of the most infamous examples of COINTELPRO's overreach was its campaign against Dr. Martin Luther King Jr. In the early 1960s, King emerged as a prominent leader of the Civil Rights Movement, advocating for nonviolent resistance to racial segregation and inequality. But to the FBI, King was seen as a dangerous radical, someone who could potentially destabilize the country. Hoover viewed King with deep suspicion, convinced that he was being influenced by communist sympathizers and that his leadership posed a threat to national security.

The FBI began a systematic campaign of surveillance and harassment against King, tapping his phones, monitoring his movements, and attempting to discredit him both publicly and privately. At one point, the FBI sent King an anonymous letter, accompanied by a tape recording of his private conversations, attempting to blackmail him into abandoning his leadership role. The letter, which insinuated that King should take his own life to avoid scandal, was a stark example of the lengths to which COINTELPRO would go in its pursuit of control.

But in trying to undermine King, the FBI only succeeded in exposing its own lack of moral authority. The public eventually learned of the FBI's attempts to sabotage the Civil Rights Movement, and far from destroying King's legacy, these revelations strengthened the resolve of activists who saw the government's actions as proof of the systemic injustice they were fighting against.

Control and Fear: Two Sides of the Same Coin

In Zen, fear is understood as one of the fundamental sources of human suffering. It arises from our attachment to things—whether those things are material possessions, relationships, or ideas. We fear losing what we hold dear, and this fear drives us to cling even more tightly to what we cannot ultimately control. But Zen teaches that fear is not something to be avoided or suppressed; rather, it must be confronted and understood. Only by facing our fears head-on can we begin to loosen the grip they have on us.

The FBI's actions during COINTELPRO were driven by fear. The fear of social change, the fear of losing power, and the fear of the unknown all contributed to the bureau's increasingly desperate attempts to control the country's political landscape. But in clinging to control, the FBI only exacerbated its own

ZEN AND THE ART OF COINTELPRO

fears. The more the bureau sought to suppress dissent, the more it became trapped in a cycle of paranoia and overreach. COINTELPRO's operations were often based on worst-case scenarios—what if the Black Panthers were planning an armed revolution? What if the anti-war movement led to widespread civil unrest?—and these fears fueled increasingly extreme actions.

From a Zen perspective, the FBI's attempts to control society were doomed to failure because they were based on an attachment to a fixed idea of how the world should be. Zen teaches that the world is constantly in flux, and that true wisdom comes from accepting this impermanence rather than resisting it. The FBI, by contrast, operated from a position of rigidity, viewing social movements not as natural expressions of change but as threats to be neutralized.

Surveillance, as practiced by COINTELPRO, was not an act of wisdom, but of fear. It was rooted in the belief that by watching and manipulating others, the government could control the course of history. But history, like all things, is impermanent. No amount of surveillance or repression could stop the tide of social change that was sweeping the country. The movements targeted by COINTELPRO—the Civil Rights Movement, the Black Power movement, the anti-war movement—were born out of the same impermanence that Zen teaches us to accept. They were responses to the injustices and inequalities of the time, and their emergence was a natural part of the shifting social landscape.

The Cost of Control: Suffering for All

STEVE SHORT

In Zen, one of the core teachings is that attachment leads to suffering. When we become attached to an outcome, a belief, or a sense of control, we set ourselves up for disappointment because the world is inherently unpredictable. This principle can be applied not only to individuals but also to institutions like the FBI.

COINTELPRO's obsession with control came at a great cost—not just to the movements it targeted, but also to the FBI itself and to society as a whole. The paranoia that infected the bureau spread to other areas of government, contributing to a culture of mistrust and fear that persists to this day. The revelations about COINTELPRO's illegal activities led to a public outcry and significant damage to the FBI's reputation. Congressional investigations in the 1970s revealed the extent of the bureau's abuses, leading to reforms aimed at curbing future overreach. But the damage had been done.

For the activists targeted by COINTELPRO, the cost of the FBI's surveillance and sabotage was often personal and devastating. Many leaders were harassed, blackmailed, or driven to despair by the constant pressure. Some, like Fred Hampton of the Black Panther Party, were killed in raids that were, at least in part, the result of FBI involvement. The fear and suspicion sown by COINTELPRO fractured movements and communities, leading to mistrust and internal conflict.

But the suffering caused by COINTELPRO was not limited to its victims. The FBI, too, suffered from its attachment to control. The bureau's internal culture became warped by paranoia, and its mission of protecting the American people was undermined by its own actions. The illusion of control, once shattered, left behind a trail of disillusionment and mistrust that has continued to haunt the agency.

Letting Go: The Zen Alternative

In contrast to COINTELPRO's obsession with control, Zen offers a path of letting go. Instead of clinging to the illusion of control, Zen teaches us to embrace the impermanence of life and to find peace in the present moment. This does not mean passivity or indifference, but rather a deep acceptance of the way things are.

For the FBI and other institutions of power, the lesson of Zen is that true security does not come from surveillance or manipulation, but from understanding and compassion. Fear can only be overcome by facing it directly, not by trying to control the world around us. The movements targeted by COINTELPRO were expressions of a deeper human yearning for justice and equality—forces that cannot be controlled, but must be understood and respected.

As we move forward into a world where surveillance is more pervasive than ever, the teachings of Zen remind us that the more we try to control, the more we will find ourselves trapped in fear and suffering. True wisdom lies in letting go, in accepting the impermanence of life, and in finding peace in the midst of change. Only then can we begin to move beyond the illusion of control and toward a more compassionate and enlightened way of being.

Mindfulness Under Surveillance

We live in an era where the lines between privacy and surveillance have blurred. Every click, every search, and every conversation has the potential to be monitored, recorded, and scrutinized by forces we often cannot see. The world of COINTELPRO, the FBI's infamous Counter Intelligence Program, may seem like a relic of the past—a chapter of history in which the government spied on its own citizens, disrupted civil rights movements, and manipulated public opinion. But the legacy of COINTELPRO lives on, not only in the broader scope of state surveillance but also in the psychological experience of living under constant watch.

In the face of this omnipresent gaze, how can one practice mindfulness, a core tenet of Zen Buddhism? Zen teaches us to stay present, to accept the reality of each moment without judgment, and to cultivate awareness of ourselves and the world around us. Yet, the question arises: what does it mean to be fully present when every action could be observed by an external force, be it governmental or corporate? How does one maintain mental freedom when external forces seek to control, manipulate, or even repress?

This chapter explores the tension between mindfulness and surveillance, using historical examples from the COINTELPRO era to illustrate the pressures activists faced under watchful eyes. These stories will serve as a backdrop for a broader exploration of how Zen principles, particularly mindfulness, can offer a powerful response to the psychological pressures of living in a surveillance state. It argues that mindfulness, far from being a passive retreat from the world, can serve as a form of resistance—an act of reclaiming mental freedom even when external control is pervasive.

The Gaze of Surveillance

To understand the challenge of mindfulness under surveillance, we must first examine what it means to live under constant observation. Surveillance, by its very nature, induces a state of hyper-awareness in those who are being watched. The knowledge that one's actions are being scrutinized, possibly judged, creates a psychological burden. Activists during the COINTELPRO era experienced this firsthand, as they became aware that their every move could be monitored, their conversations tapped, their associates infiltrated. In many cases, this led to deep feelings of paranoia, mistrust, and anxiety.

COINTELPRO was, in essence, a tool of psychological warfare. The FBI's goal was not just to physically disrupt movements like the Civil Rights Movement or the Black Panther Party, but to create an environment of fear and uncertainty that would paralyze individuals from within. Activists were led to believe that they could not trust anyone, that every person around them could be an informant, and that every step they took could lead to their downfall.

In a similar vein, the modern surveillance state, with its extensive network of cameras, data collection, and digital monitoring, creates a pervasive sense of being watched. While the technology may have evolved, the psychological impact remains the same. The fear of surveillance leads to self-censorship, the curbing of free expression, and a narrowing of one's sense of personal autonomy. In a world where privacy is compromised, many feel as though their every action must be calculated and controlled. This pressure to conform to expectations, to avoid attracting unwanted attention, can cause a disconnection from the self.

Zen and the Reality of the Moment

Mindfulness, at its core, is about being fully present in the here and now. In Zen, mindfulness is not just a mental exercise but a way of living—a commitment to being deeply aware of one's thoughts, emotions, and surroundings without becoming attached to them. It is about accepting reality as it is, without resistance or judgment, even when that reality is uncomfortable or threatening.

The practice of mindfulness can serve as a powerful counterbalance to the psychological effects of surveillance. While surveillance induces fear and a sense of disempowerment, mindfulness encourages us to reclaim our mental space, to become observers of our own experience rather than passive victims of external forces. In a sense, mindfulness creates a "space" within oneself that is inviolable—a mental sanctuary that cannot be penetrated by surveillance, no matter how pervasive.

To practice mindfulness under surveillance is to cultivate a kind of inner freedom, one that is not contingent upon external circumstances. It is the freedom to choose how we respond to the knowledge that we are being watched, the freedom to remain present and grounded even when external forces seek to destabilize us. This is not to say that surveillance should be passively accepted, but rather that mindfulness can give individuals the psychological tools to resist its most insidious effects: fear, anxiety, and self-censorship.

Zen teaches that the present moment is all that truly exists. The past is gone, the future is yet to come, and the only reality we can engage with is the now. Surveillance, on the other hand, creates a future-oriented fear—an anxiety about what might happen as a result of being observed. Will this action be used against me? Will this association lead to consequences? Mindfulness, by contrast, encourages us to release these fears and to focus on the present, where true agency resides.

The Activist's Dilemma: Freedom Under Watch

For activists during the COINTELPRO era, the tension between action and surveillance was palpable. Take the case of Fred Hampton, the charismatic leader of the Illinois chapter of the Black Panther Party. Hampton, at just 21 years old, was a powerful orator and organizer, uniting diverse communities under a vision of economic and social justice. Yet, he was also under constant FBI surveillance, targeted for "neutralization" as part of COINTELPRO's efforts to disrupt the Black Panthers.

Despite the knowledge that he was being watched, Hampton continued his work, organizing breakfast programs for children, community clinics, and educational initiatives. His awareness of the surveillance did not paralyze him, but it undoubtedly added a layer of psychological pressure. Tragically, Hampton was assassinated by the Chicago police in 1969, an event orchestrated with information provided by an FBI informant.

Hampton's life, and his ultimate death, raise profound questions about how one maintains a sense of freedom and purpose under constant watch. While Hampton's activism was cut short, his legacy endures as a testament to the power of staying true to one's principles, even in the face of overwhelming repression. His story illustrates the difficulty—and the importance—of remaining mindful and present in the face of external forces that seek to control not just actions, but minds.

For activists today, whether in movements for racial justice, environmental sustainability, or other causes, the lessons of COINTELPRO remain relevant. Modern-day surveillance is more technologically advanced, but its psychological impact is remarkably similar. Activists must navigate the dual realities of fighting for change while being aware that their every action may be recorded, their communications intercepted, their networks infiltrated.

In this context, mindfulness becomes a form of psychological resilience. It allows individuals to remain grounded in their purpose and values, even when they are under intense scrutiny. By focusing on the present moment and refusing to become overwhelmed by the fear of potential future consequences, activists can maintain their sense of agency and autonomy. This does not mean ignoring the risks, but rather facing them with clarity and calm.

Mindfulness as Resistance

Mindfulness, as understood in the Zen tradition, is not a retreat from the world, but an active engagement with it. To be mindful is to see things as they are, to cut through illusion and distraction, and to confront reality head-on. In this sense, mindfulness can be a form of resistance—resistance to the forces of control, manipulation, and surveillance that seek to dominate our minds.

One of the key insights of Zen is the concept of *non-attachment*. In the context of surveillance, this does not mean detaching from the reality of being watched, but rather detaching from the fear and anxiety that surveillance seeks to instill. Surveillance, by its nature, tries to create a sense of powerlessness in the observed, a feeling that one's autonomy is being stripped away. Mindfulness, on the other hand, reminds us that true power lies within—the power to choose how we respond to our circumstances.

In a surveillance state, the ultimate act of resistance may be to refuse to internalize the fear that is being imposed. To live mindfully is to reclaim one's inner freedom, to remain centered in the face of external pressure. This inner freedom is not something that can be taken away by cameras, wiretaps, or data collection. It exists in the space between stimulus and response, in the quiet awareness of the present moment.

Mindfulness also allows individuals to see through the tactics of surveillance. The goal of COINTELPRO, and of many modern surveillance programs, is to create self-policing individuals—people who modify their behavior out of fear of being watched. By staying mindful, by remaining aware of the present moment without succumbing to fear or paranoia, individuals can resist this internalized control. They can continue to act according to their values and principles, even in the face of external scrutiny.

The Mindful Response to Fear

Fear is one of the most powerful tools of control. Governments and institutions have long used fear to manipulate behavior, to suppress dissent, and to maintain power. Surveillance, in many ways, is a mechanism for instilling fear—the fear of being caught, the fear of being judged, the fear of consequences. COINTELPRO, with its covert tactics and secret files, relied heavily on this kind of psychological intimidation.

Zen offers a different approach to fear. Rather than avoiding or suppressing fear, Zen teaches us to confront it directly. Mindfulness allows us to observe our fear without becoming consumed by it. In meditation, we may experience fear as a sensation in the body—tightness in the chest, a quickening of the breath—but rather than trying to push it away, we simply observe it. In this way, fear loses its power over us. It becomes just another passing emotion, impermanent like all things.

For those living under surveillance, whether activists or ordinary citizens, mindfulness can provide a way to face the fear that surveillance generates. By staying present and accepting the reality of being watched, we can begin to disarm the fear that surveillance seeks to instill. This does not mean becoming indifferent to the dangers of surveillance, but rather refusing to let fear dictate our actions.

Reclaiming Mental Freedom

In a world where surveillance is becoming ever more pervasive, mindfulness offers a path to reclaiming mental freedom. By staying present, by accepting the reality of each moment without judgment, and by refusing to internalize the fear that surveillance seeks to impose, individuals can resist the psychological pressures of living under watch. The practice of mindfulness allows us to cultivate inner freedom, even when external forces seek to control us.

The lessons of Zen are not just about finding peace in isolation; they are about engaging with the world in a way that is mindful, compassionate, and courageous. In the face of surveillance, mindfulness becomes an act of resistance—a way to remain true to ourselves and our values, even when we are being watched. This inner freedom is something that no government, no institution, and no surveillance program can take away.

The challenge of mindfulness under surveillance is ultimately a challenge of how we live our lives in a world that often seeks to control us. By embracing mindfulness, we can reclaim our autonomy, resist the forces of fear and control, and find peace in the present moment. In this way, we move beyond the illusion of control and towards a deeper, more meaningful freedom.

COINTELPRO's Karmic Consequences

In Zen and broader Buddhist philosophy, the principle of karma stands as a central tenet of the moral universe. Karma, derived from the Sanskrit word meaning "action" or "deed," carries with it the understanding that every action has consequences that ripple outward, affecting both the individual and the collective in ways that may not be immediately apparent. Karma is not a punitive or reward system but a natural law of cause and effect, intimately tied to the interconnectedness of all beings. In this sense, one's actions have ethical consequences that can shape the trajectory of their life and the world around them.

As we apply this principle to the actions of COINTELPRO, the FBI's covert Counter Intelligence Program, we can begin to see how the program's operations—designed to surveil, disrupt, and neutralize political movements—produced lasting karmic ripples. While the immediate effects of COINTELPRO were often concrete and devastating—arrests, dismantled organizations, deaths—the long-term consequences are more insidious and pervasive. Distrust in institutions, fractured social movements, and psychological damage to the individuals targeted are just a few of the long-lasting consequences. In this chapter, we will explore how the karmic consequences of COINTELPRO reverberate through society, long after the program itself was officially dismantled.

STEVE SHORT

COINTELPRO: Seeds of Distrust

COINTELPRO's operations began in the late 1950s, initially targeting communist organizations during the height of the Cold War. However, by the 1960s, its scope expanded to include a wide range of domestic political movements, from civil rights groups like the Southern Christian Leadership Conference (SCLC) to the Black Panther Party, feminist organizations, and the anti-Vietnam War movement. The FBI, under the leadership of J. Edgar Hoover, saw these groups as threats to the established social and political order. COINTELPRO aimed to neutralize these movements through surveillance, infiltration, disinformation campaigns, and, in some cases, direct sabotage.

The FBI justified these actions in the name of national security, framing dissent as subversion and protest as a precursor to domestic upheaval. However, the methods employed by COINTELPRO—covert, manipulative, and often illegal—sowed the seeds of deep distrust in government institutions. Once the public became aware of the FBI's covert operations, particularly through the release of internal documents in 1971, the fallout was significant. Activists, scholars, and ordinary citizens began to question the integrity of the FBI, and by extension, other branches of government. What other unconstitutional actions had been taken under the guise of protecting democracy? Could any institution be trusted?

This distrust is one of COINTELPRO's most enduring legacies. Even today, many Americans view the government

ZEN AND THE ART OF COINTELPRO

with skepticism, especially when it comes to issues of surveillance, policing, and civil liberties. The karmic consequences of COINTELPRO's actions have persisted, creating a deep rift between citizens and their government, a rift that is continually deepened by new revelations of governmental overreach, from the NSA's mass surveillance programs to the militarization of the police in response to social movements like Black Lives Matter. In this way, COINTELPRO set a precedent for government surveillance and manipulation that has echoed through decades, poisoning the relationship between citizens and the state.

Fractured Movements, Fragmented Trust

Beyond the impact on institutional trust, the karmic ripples of COINTELPRO can be seen in the fragmentation of social movements that were targeted during its active years. One of the program's explicit goals was to sow division within activist groups, weakening their ability to organize and present a united front. The FBI employed various tactics to achieve this, from sending anonymous letters designed to stir mistrust between movement leaders, to planting informants who would exacerbate existing tensions and escalate internal conflicts.

One of the most famous examples of COINTELPRO's divisive tactics involved the Black Panther Party (BPP), one of the most heavily targeted groups. The Panthers, with their focus on community self-defense, social programs, and black empowerment, were viewed by the FBI as a significant threat. The FBI sought to weaken the BPP by exploiting the personal and political rivalries between its leaders. In one instance, the

FBI sent an anonymous letter to Eldridge Cleaver, a prominent Panther leader, suggesting that other members of the party were plotting against him. These tactics fueled existing tensions within the group, contributing to its eventual fragmentation.

The karmic consequences of these actions can still be felt today. Many social movements that arose in the wake of the civil rights era have struggled to achieve the same level of unity and cohesion. The deep mistrust and paranoia sown by COINTELPRO did not simply disappear when the program was exposed. Activist groups became more guarded, less willing to trust outsiders or even fellow members, for fear of infiltration. This has had a long-lasting effect on the ability of movements to organize effectively, to build coalitions, and to sustain momentum over time.

The divisions within movements like the Black Panthers also had a broader social impact. As these organizations weakened, so did the broader push for systemic change. COINTELPRO was successful, at least in part, in neutralizing many of the most radical elements of the 1960s and 70s social movements. The result was a splintering of activist energy, as well as a deep sense of disillusionment among many who had fought for justice and equality. The karmic ripples of this disillusionment have reverberated through generations, as activists today continue to grapple with the legacy of COINTELPRO's divide-and-conquer tactics.

Psychological Damage: The Personal Toll of COINTELPRO

ZEN AND THE ART OF COINTELPRO

While the societal and institutional consequences of COINTELPRO are significant, perhaps the most profound karmic consequences are those experienced by the individuals who were directly targeted by the program. For many activists, being the subject of government surveillance, harassment, and manipulation took a significant psychological toll. The knowledge that one's every move could be monitored, that friends and associates might be informants, and that one's personal life could be weaponized against them created an environment of constant fear and anxiety.

The psychological impact of COINTELPRO was not limited to those who were actively engaged in political movements. Family members, friends, and entire communities were affected by the pervasive atmosphere of mistrust that the program cultivated. Children of activists grew up in homes where the phone might be tapped, where visitors were viewed with suspicion, and where the constant threat of police raids or arrests loomed large. This kind of chronic stress can have long-lasting effects, contributing to anxiety disorders, depression, and other mental health issues.

Moreover, COINTELPRO's tactics of disinformation and character assassination often targeted the very core of an individual's identity. Activists like Martin Luther King Jr., who were subjected to relentless surveillance and smear campaigns, were not just attacked for their political beliefs but for their personal lives. The FBI attempted to discredit King by threatening to reveal details of his private life, a tactic designed to destroy his public image and undermine his leadership in the Civil Rights Movement. These kinds of attacks were deeply personal, designed to erode the self-worth and mental stability of their targets.

The karmic consequences of this psychological damage are far-reaching. Many individuals who were targeted by COINTELPRO struggled with the trauma of being surveilled and manipulated long after the program ended. In some cases, the psychological scars were passed down to future generations, as children of activists inherited the trauma of their parents' experiences. The pervasive sense of mistrust, anxiety, and paranoia that COINTELPRO cultivated in its targets has left a lasting imprint on both individuals and communities, shaping the way future generations engage with activism and with the government.

The Ripple Effect on Communities of Color

While COINTELPRO targeted a broad range of political movements, its most intense focus was on Black, Indigenous, and other people of color who were engaged in struggles for racial justice and self-determination. The program's operations against groups like the Black Panther Party, the American Indian Movement (AIM), and the Nation of Islam were not just about neutralizing political dissent; they were also about maintaining the racial status quo. COINTELPRO viewed movements that sought to challenge systemic racism and white supremacy as existential threats to the American social order.

The karmic consequences of COINTELPRO's operations on communities of color are profound. By targeting these movements, the FBI not only sought to suppress political organizing but also to undermine the social and cultural cohesion of marginalized communities. The disinformation campaigns, infiltration, and surveillance that COINTELPRO employed created deep fractures within these communities, exacerbating internal conflicts and creating a climate of fear and suspicion that extended beyond the political sphere.

In Black communities, for example, COINTELPRO's targeting of the Black Panther Party and other civil rights organizations contributed to the erosion of trust in leadership and the fragmentation of grassroots organizing efforts. This had long-term effects on the ability of these communities to mobilize for social change. The karmic consequences of this disruption are still evident today, as communities of color continue to face significant challenges in organizing for racial justice in the face of ongoing surveillance, policing, and state repression.

Moreover, COINTELPRO's targeting of Black and Indigenous leaders reinforced a narrative of criminality and danger that has continued to shape the way these communities are perceived and treated by law enforcement and the broader society. The legacy of COINTELPRO's criminalization of Black and Indigenous activism can be seen in the ongoing struggles against police violence, mass incarceration, and systemic racism. The karmic ripples of these actions continue to reverberate, as the descendants of those targeted by COINTELPRO continue to bear the brunt of state violence and repression.

Ethical Consequences: The FBI's Karma

STEVE SHORT

Just as individuals and communities have experienced the karmic consequences of COINTELPRO, so too has the FBI. While the program was designed to protect the state and maintain order, its covert and often illegal tactics have had a lasting impact on the bureau's reputation and legacy. The exposure of COINTELPRO in the early 1970s led to widespread public outrage, congressional hearings, and reforms within the FBI. However, the damage to the bureau's credibility was done.

In many ways, COINTELPRO became a symbol of the dangers of unchecked government power. The ethical consequences of the program have haunted the FBI for decades, as it continues to grapple with the legacy of its past abuses. The bureau's involvement in political repression has made it difficult for many Americans, particularly those from marginalized communities, to trust law enforcement or believe in the FBI's commitment to justice and fairness.

The karmic lesson for the FBI is clear: actions taken out of fear, control, and manipulation ultimately come back to haunt those who engage in them. The bureau's attempts to suppress dissent and maintain control over the social order have created long-lasting distrust, both in the FBI itself and in the broader institutions of government. This distrust continues to shape the political landscape, as activists, civil rights groups, and ordinary citizens remain wary of government surveillance and interference.

The Long Shadow of COINTELPRO

ZEN AND THE ART OF COINTELPRO

The karmic consequences of COINTELPRO are vast and multifaceted. From the erosion of trust in government institutions to the fragmentation of social movements and the lasting psychological damage to individuals and communities, the program's legacy is one of profound ethical and social repercussions. Just as in Zen philosophy, where every action creates ripples that extend far beyond the immediate moment, COINTELPRO's actions continue to reverberate through American society.

In exploring these karmic consequences, we are reminded of the interconnectedness of all beings and the profound impact that our actions can have on the world around us. COINTELPRO's legacy is a cautionary tale about the dangers of seeking control through fear and manipulation. It serves as a reminder that the quest for dominance and power, no matter how well-intentioned, inevitably leads to suffering—for both those who seek control and those who are subjected to it.

As we reflect on the karmic consequences of COINTELPRO, we are called to consider the ethical implications of surveillance, repression, and state power in our own time. The lessons of the past can guide us as we seek to build a more just, compassionate, and mindful society—one where the principles of freedom, justice, and equality are not sacrificed in the name of control.

The Weaponization of Fear

Fear has always been one of the most potent weapons in human history. From oppressive regimes to social control tactics, fear has been used to manipulate, intimidate, and paralyze individuals and entire populations. The FBI's COINTELPRO (Counter Intelligence Program) understood this all too well and thrived on fear—fear of social change, fear of revolution, and fear of "the other." Through COINTELPRO, the FBI harnessed fear as a tool to destabilize movements that challenged the status quo. From disinformation campaigns to intimidation tactics and the deliberate sowing of discord, COINTELPRO systematically exploited the human psychological tendency to respond to fear with paralysis, suspicion, and division.

In Zen philosophy, however, fear is understood very differently. While the FBI sought to weaponize fear for control, Zen teaches that fear is a mental construct, an illusion created by the mind. According to Zen, fear is not an inherent force in the world but a product of our attachment to ideas, identities, and expectations. By practicing detachment and mindfulness, we can dissolve fear and see it for what it truly is: a transient emotion, born of our mind's grasping for control.

In this chapter, we will explore the weaponization of fear by COINTELPRO, examining the psychological tactics employed by the FBI to dismantle social movements. At the same time, we will delve into the Zen concept of fear as an illusion and how mindfulness practices can help dissolve fear, offering a way to resist its manipulation. By juxtaposing these two perspectives, we invite readers to consider how fear can be both weaponized in society and transcended through mindful awareness.

The Power of Fear in COINTELPRO's Tactics

COINTELPRO was built on the premise of fear—fear of Communism, fear of Black empowerment, fear of anti-war movements, and fear of any group that dared to challenge the political and social establishment. The FBI, under J. Edgar Hoover's leadership, viewed these movements as existential threats to the American way of life. But rather than confront these movements in open, democratic ways, COINTELPRO relied on covert operations designed to sow fear and confusion within activist circles.

One of COINTELPRO's primary tools was disinformation. The FBI routinely spread false information, fabricated documents, and forged letters to create distrust among movement leaders and their followers. For example, in the case of the Black Panther Party (BPP), the FBI sent anonymous letters to key members, suggesting that others in the leadership were plotting against them. These letters played on pre-existing tensions within the organization, stoking fears of betrayal and internal power struggles. By amplifying these fears, the FBI effectively weakened the unity and resolve of the BPP, which was already under pressure from external forces such as police harassment and economic deprivation.

The FBI also employed intimidation tactics designed to instill fear directly into the hearts of activists. Members of the Civil Rights Movement, the American Indian Movement (AIM), and other targeted groups were subjected to constant surveillance, harassment, and threats. Homes were raided in the middle of the night, phone lines were tapped, and agents would sometimes even send anonymous death threats. These actions were meant not only to terrorize individuals but also to create a broader climate of fear, where activists would feel constantly watched, hunted, and vulnerable. Fear, in this context, became a paralyzing force, undermining the confidence and morale of those working for change.

By sowing discord and fear, the FBI hoped to prevent movements from achieving their goals. Activists were led to question not only their safety but also their allies and even their purpose. Fear turned solidarity into suspicion, collaboration into competition, and boldness into caution. In the face of such fear, movements often struggled to maintain the unity and clarity necessary to continue their work. This was exactly what COINTELPRO intended: fear as a means to divide, conquer, and maintain control.

Zen's Understanding of Fear: A Mental Construct

In contrast to COINTELPRO's deliberate weaponization of fear, Zen philosophy teaches that fear itself is an illusion, a construct of the mind. In Zen, the mind is seen as the source of suffering, because it is constantly grasping, attaching, and identifying with thoughts and emotions. Fear arises when the mind becomes attached to a particular outcome or identity,

ZEN AND THE ART OF COINTELPRO

when it perceives a threat to what it clings to. Whether it is fear of death, fear of failure, or fear of the unknown, Zen teaches that all fear stems from this attachment.

Zen practitioners are taught to view fear not as something to be avoided or fought, but as something to be observed and understood. Fear, like all emotions, is transient and impermanent. It arises, lingers for a time, and then passes away. By practicing mindfulness, one can observe the arising of fear in the mind without becoming entangled in it. Through this detached observation, fear loses its power. It is seen for what it truly is: a momentary flicker in the ever-changing landscape of consciousness.

The Zen concept of detachment is key to dissolving fear. When we detach from the need to control outcomes, when we let go of our attachment to ideas of safety, identity, or success, fear begins to dissipate. This is not to say that danger disappears or that one becomes indifferent to risks. Rather, Zen teaches us to accept the present moment as it is, without allowing fear to cloud our perception or dictate our actions. Fear, when observed mindfully, becomes just another passing sensation, no different from joy, sadness, or any other emotion.

In the context of activism and resistance, this Zen approach to fear offers a powerful tool for resilience. COINTELPRO relied on fear to destabilize movements, but activists who can recognize fear as an illusion and practice detachment are less vulnerable to such manipulation. By cultivating mindfulness and presence, individuals and movements can maintain their clarity, purpose, and solidarity even in the face of intense psychological pressure.

The Psychological Tactics of COINTELPRO

COINTELPRO's psychological tactics were finely tuned to exploit the vulnerabilities of the human mind, particularly the fear of isolation and betrayal. By tapping into these deep-seated fears, the FBI was able to create divisions within movements that might otherwise have remained strong. One of the most effective strategies COINTELPRO employed was the use of "snitch jacketing"—the deliberate spread of rumors that a key activist was an informant for the FBI. This tactic played on the fear of betrayal, a fear that is almost universal in tight-knit activist communities.

The fear of betrayal is rooted in the fundamental human need for trust and connection. When activists work together in dangerous and often illegal activities, trust becomes a vital part of their relationships. The idea that one of their own could be working against them, secretly feeding information to the government, creates a deep sense of insecurity and paranoia. By spreading rumors of informants, COINTELPRO fostered an atmosphere of suspicion and mistrust, weakening the bonds that held movements together.

Another psychological tactic employed by COINTELPRO was the use of personal attacks to undermine the credibility of movement leaders. Martin Luther King Jr., for example, was subjected to a relentless campaign of surveillance and harassment. The FBI attempted to discredit King by gathering information about his personal life and then using it to threaten him. In one infamous incident, the FBI sent an anonymous letter to King, along with recordings of his alleged extramarital affairs, suggesting that he should commit suicide to avoid public disgrace.

These personal attacks were designed to create fear and self-doubt in movement leaders. By threatening to expose their personal vulnerabilities, the FBI sought to undermine their confidence and authority, both within the movement and in the public eye. This tactic was particularly insidious because it preyed on the human fear of shame and public humiliation, fears that are deeply ingrained in our social consciousness.

Fear as a Tool of Social Control

COINTELPRO's use of fear was not unique to the FBI. Governments and institutions throughout history have used fear as a tool of social control, particularly in times of political unrest or social change. Fear can be used to justify authoritarian measures, to suppress dissent, and to manipulate public opinion. In the case of COINTELPRO, the FBI capitalized on the fears of the American public—fears of Communism, race riots, and radical social change—to justify its covert operations. By framing social movements as threats to national security, the FBI was able to generate public support for its repressive actions.

This use of fear as a tool of social control is deeply rooted in human psychology. Fear is a primal emotion, one that can override reason and logic. When people are afraid, they are more likely to accept authoritarian measures, even at the expense of their own freedoms. This is why fear is such an effective tool for those in power—it can be used to manipulate individuals and entire populations into compliance.

Zen philosophy, however, offers a counter-narrative to this use of fear. While governments and institutions may seek to control through fear, Zen teaches that true freedom comes from within. Fear, when observed mindfully, loses its power to control us. By practicing detachment, we can free ourselves from the grip of fear and make decisions based on wisdom and compassion, rather than on the desire for safety or security.

Dissolving Fear through Mindfulness

In a world where fear is weaponized for control, how can individuals resist its effects? Zen offers a simple yet profound answer: mindfulness. Through the practice of mindfulness, we can learn to observe fear without becoming consumed by it. When fear arises, we do not need to react immediately. Instead, we can pause, breathe, and simply notice the sensation of fear in the body and mind. This act of observation creates a space between the stimulus (the fear-inducing event) and our response to it. In this space, we regain our agency and can choose how to respond, rather than reacting out of fear.

Zen teacher Thich Nhat Hanh often spoke of mindfulness as a way of "coming home" to ourselves. When we are fully present in the moment, we are no longer at the mercy of our thoughts, fears, and emotions. Mindfulness allows us to see clearly, to act from a place of wisdom rather than from a place of fear.

ZEN AND THE ART OF COINTELPRO

In the context of activism, this means that we can continue to work for justice and change even in the face of surveillance, harassment, and repression. Fear loses its power when we refuse to be controlled by it.

Fear as an Illusion

COINTELPRO thrived on fear because fear is such a potent force in the human psyche. By exploiting our fears of betrayal, isolation, and shame, the FBI was able to undermine movements that sought to create a more just and equitable society. However, Zen teaches us that fear is not a fixed reality; it is an illusion, a mental construct that can be dissolved through mindfulness and detachment.

In a world where fear is often weaponized for control, the practice of mindfulness offers a path to freedom. By observing fear without becoming entangled in it, we can maintain our clarity, purpose, and resolve. We can continue to work for justice, even in the face of fear, knowing that fear itself is just another passing moment in the ever-changing flow of life.

The weaponization of fear may be a powerful tool for those in power, but the Zen practitioner knows that true freedom lies not in avoiding fear, but in seeing through it. By recognizing fear as an illusion, we can transcend its power and continue to act with courage and compassion in the face of adversity.

The Zen of Subversion

Subversion, in its most basic form, means to undermine authority or power, often through covert or manipulative means. The FBI's COINTELPRO (Counter Intelligence Program) was a state-sponsored exercise in subversion, specifically targeting social movements that threatened the established order of American society. Through surveillance, manipulation, and psychological warfare, COINTELPRO aimed to dismantle progressive movements from the inside out, undermining their leadership, creating distrust among members, and ultimately neutralizing their potential for change.

However, COINTELPRO's methods of subversion—steeped in fear, paranoia, and manipulation—are in direct contrast to the principles of Zen. Zen teaches that subversion of unjust power structures does not come from violence, secret operations, or psychological games. Rather, true subversion lies in the cultivation of peace, equanimity, and compassion in the face of oppression. In Zen, the most powerful way to undermine fear, control, and oppression is to embody the very principles that these forces seek to extinguish—kindness, mindfulness, and love. It is in the stillness of the mind and the refusal to be controlled by fear that the most profound form of subversion takes place.

This chapter explores the concept of subversion from a Zen perspective, challenging the traditional understanding of subversion as a clandestine act of rebellion. Instead, it offers

ZEN AND THE ART OF COINTELPRO

the argument that true subversion is found in the ability to maintain peace and inner freedom, even in the face of overwhelming external control. Through historical examples of activists who resisted COINTELPRO not with violence or deception but with love, compassion, and mindful resistance, this chapter delves into the transformative power of Zen principles as tools for social change.

COINTELPRO's Subversive Tactics

COINTELPRO was, by design, a program of subversion. Its primary objective was to infiltrate and disrupt social movements that sought to challenge the dominant power structures in the United States during the mid-20th century. The movements targeted by COINTELPRO included the Civil Rights Movement, the Black Panther Party, the American Indian Movement (AIM), and various anti-Vietnam War and feminist organizations. These movements were seen as threats to the established order, and the FBI sought to neutralize them by any means necessary.

The FBI's approach to subversion was multifaceted. First, it relied on surveillance—constant observation of leaders, activists, and organizations. Through wiretaps, informants, and undercover agents, the FBI gathered intelligence on movement activities, internal dynamics, and individual vulnerabilities. This intelligence was then used to create internal conflict, exploit weaknesses, and spread disinformation. By turning movement members against one another, the FBI hoped to create divisions that would undermine the movements from within.

STEVE SHORT

A key tactic employed by COINTELPRO was "snitch jacketing," or falsely labeling a movement leader or member as an informant. This tactic played on the fear and paranoia already present within activist communities, many of which were aware of the state's efforts to infiltrate their ranks. By creating the perception that certain individuals were working with the FBI, COINTELPRO sowed distrust and disunity, leading to the isolation and marginalization of key leaders. This tactic was used against figures like Black Panther leaders Huey Newton and Eldridge Cleaver, exacerbating pre-existing tensions within the organization.

Another method of subversion was psychological harassment. The FBI would send anonymous letters, make threatening phone calls, and engage in smear campaigns to destabilize movement leaders. Martin Luther King Jr. was a prime target of this psychological warfare. In one particularly infamous case, the FBI sent King an anonymous letter urging him to commit suicide, accompanied by recordings of his alleged extramarital affairs. This tactic aimed to discredit King in the eyes of the public and create personal turmoil that would detract from his leadership in the Civil Rights Movement.

COINTELPRO's subversion was rooted in fear—fear of social change, fear of empowered marginalized communities, and fear of revolution. The program relied on covert operations, manipulation, and deceit to achieve its goals, creating a climate of suspicion and paranoia. But as we shall see, these methods of subversion, while temporarily effective in some cases, ultimately failed to crush the movements they targeted. This is because true subversion—subversion that transforms society

ZEN AND THE ART OF COINTELPRO

and consciousness—cannot be achieved through manipulation and fear. It requires a deeper, more spiritual approach.

The Zen Perspective on Subversion

In Zen, subversion is not about undermining others through covert operations or psychological manipulation. Rather, it is about subverting the forces of fear, attachment, and delusion within oneself. Zen teaches that true freedom comes from within, and that external power structures only have control over us to the extent that we allow them to. The mind is the seat of suffering, according to Zen, because it clings to desires, fears, and identities. By letting go of these attachments, we become free from suffering, and in doing so, we undermine the very foundations of control that external authorities rely on.

From a Zen perspective, the most radical form of subversion is the refusal to be controlled by fear. In a surveillance state, where the government monitors every move, it is easy to become consumed by anxiety and paranoia. But Zen teaches that these emotions are constructs of the mind, and by practicing mindfulness, we can observe them without becoming attached to them. This practice of non-attachment allows us to remain calm and centered, even in the face of external oppression.

Zen also emphasizes the importance of compassion in the face of aggression. While COINTELPRO sought to destroy movements through fear and division, Zen teaches that the most powerful response to hatred is love. This is not a passive love, but a fierce, courageous love that refuses to be diminished by oppression. When we respond to violence with compassion, we subvert the very logic of oppression, which relies on creating cycles of fear, hatred, and retaliation. By breaking this cycle, we create the possibility for true transformation—both within ourselves and within society.

Historical Moments of Zen-Like Subversion

Throughout history, there have been countless examples of individuals and movements that embodied the Zen principles of peace, equanimity, and compassion in their resistance to oppression. These acts of mindful resistance subverted COINTELPRO's efforts to control and destroy movements, showing that true subversion comes not from violence or deceit, but from the unwavering commitment to justice, love, and inner freedom.

One powerful example of this Zen-like subversion is found in the life of Dr. Martin Luther King Jr. While King may not have been a Zen practitioner, his philosophy of nonviolence and love in the face of hatred echoes Zen principles. King's commitment to nonviolent resistance was not just a political strategy—it was a spiritual practice. He believed that love was the most powerful force in the universe, and that responding to hatred with love would ultimately transform both the oppressor and the oppressed.

COINTELPRO's attempts to discredit and destroy King were relentless. The FBI tapped his phones, spread disinformation about his personal life, and tried to turn members of his inner circle against him. But despite these efforts, King remained

ZEN AND THE ART OF COINTELPRO

steadfast in his commitment to nonviolence and love. In his famous "Letter from Birmingham Jail," King wrote, "Injustice anywhere is a threat to justice everywhere." His words reflected a deep understanding of interconnectedness—a core Zen principle—and his ability to maintain equanimity in the face of relentless oppression was a profound act of subversion.

Another example of mindful resistance comes from the Black Panther Party, which was one of COINTELPRO's primary targets. The Panthers, often depicted as militant and violent by the mainstream media, also engaged in profound acts of compassion and community building. The Panthers' free breakfast programs, health clinics, and educational initiatives were designed to uplift marginalized communities and provide services that the government had failed to offer. These acts of care and compassion were a direct subversion of the state's attempts to portray the Panthers as violent extremists.

While COINTELPRO sought to undermine the Panthers through fear and manipulation, the Panthers' commitment to their communities demonstrated a different kind of power—the power of collective care. By providing food, healthcare, and education to those in need, the Panthers subverted the logic of the state, which relied on neglecting and marginalizing Black communities. Their work showed that true power comes not from dominating others, but from serving and caring for them.

The American Indian Movement (AIM) also provides a powerful example of mindful resistance. AIM, which sought to address the historical and ongoing injustices faced by Native

American communities, was another major target of COINTELPRO. The FBI infiltrated AIM, spread false information, and engaged in violent repression, particularly during the Wounded Knee Occupation of 1973. Despite this intense pressure, AIM leaders like Dennis Banks and Russell Means continued to advocate for Native sovereignty and the rights of Indigenous peoples.

AIM's resistance was rooted in a deep spiritual connection to the land and the ancestors, a connection that echoes Zen principles of interconnectedness and mindfulness. By grounding their resistance in this spiritual foundation, AIM leaders were able to maintain a sense of purpose and peace, even in the face of state violence. Their commitment to nonviolent resistance and the protection of sacred lands was a profound act of subversion against a government that sought to erase Indigenous cultures and histories.

Mindful Resistance as Subversion

Mindful resistance is the practice of engaging in activism and social change from a place of inner peace, clarity, and compassion. It is the embodiment of Zen principles in the realm of social justice, and it offers a powerful alternative to the violence and fear that often accompany struggles for change. Mindful resistance is not about defeating the enemy through force, but about transforming the very conditions that give rise to oppression.

In the context of COINTELPRO, mindful resistance takes on particular significance. While the FBI sought to destroy

ZEN AND THE ART OF COINTELPRO

movements through fear and manipulation, mindful activists were able to maintain their integrity, compassion, and sense of purpose. By refusing to be controlled by fear, these activists subverted COINTELPRO's tactics and created the conditions for lasting change.

The Zen of subversion is about more than just resisting oppression—it is about transforming the self and society through mindfulness, compassion, and equanimity. It is about cultivating a deep sense of inner freedom that cannot be touched by external forces, no matter how powerful they may seem. This form of subversion is not flashy or violent, but it is deeply transformative.

In a world where fear and manipulation are often used as tools of control, the practice of mindful resistance offers a path to true liberation. By embodying peace, compassion, and mindfulness, we can subvert the very forces that seek to oppress us. And in doing so, we can create a world where justice, love, and inner freedom are the foundation of our collective existence.

Emptiness and the FBI Files

At the heart of Zen philosophy lies the concept of "emptiness" (Śūnyatā), which points to the impermanence and interdependence of all things. In Buddhist thought, emptiness does not imply nihilism or the absence of meaning; rather, it reflects the idea that all phenomena are void of inherent, unchanging essence. Everything is interconnected, constantly in flux, and subject to change. Understanding this principle allows one to transcend the illusions of permanence and separateness that often bind the mind.

In a completely different realm, the same notion of emptiness can be strikingly observed in the FBI's redacted files from COINTELPRO, where entire pages are blacked out, names are scrubbed, and entire operations are shrouded in secrecy. These files, despite being officially declassified, retain a haunting emptiness—one born not from spiritual insight but from the deliberate concealment of information. The absence of transparency in these heavily censored documents points to a type of bureaucratic emptiness, one designed to obscure rather than reveal, to confuse rather than enlighten.

This chapter will explore the intersection between Zen's concept of emptiness and the literal emptiness found in COINTELPRO files, weaving together themes of ignorance, secrecy, and hidden truths. What does it mean to engage with a history that has been deliberately erased or obscured? How can we seek truth in a world where information is manipulated and controlled by those in power? And what does the nature of

ZEN AND THE ART OF COINTELPRO

emptiness teach us about our relationship to truth, knowledge, and the unknown?

The Nature of Emptiness in Zen

In Zen Buddhism, emptiness is often misunderstood by those unfamiliar with the concept. It is not about nothingness or void, but about recognizing the lack of fixed, inherent nature in all things. Everything is interconnected and exists in relation to something else. For example, a tree exists in relation to the earth, the sun, water, and countless other factors. There is no separate, permanent "tree" essence—only a collection of processes and conditions that come together temporarily. In this way, all phenomena are "empty" of a separate, permanent identity.

This idea extends to our own minds and identities. The self, according to Zen, is not a fixed entity but a fluid collection of thoughts, emotions, memories, and experiences that are constantly changing. The belief in a permanent self is an illusion, and clinging to that illusion is a source of suffering. Zen practice aims to help individuals see through this illusion, to realize the emptiness of the self, and to live in harmony with the ever-changing nature of reality.

Emptiness, therefore, is not a negative or frightening concept; it is a liberating insight into the nature of existence. It allows us to let go of attachment to fixed ideas, rigid identities, and the desire for control. In doing so, we open ourselves to a more expansive and compassionate way of being in the world.

The Literal Emptiness of FBI Files

STEVE SHORT

When we turn our attention to the declassified FBI files from the COINTELPRO era, we encounter another form of emptiness, though one that carries a very different meaning. These documents are full of redactions—blacked-out names, entire sentences obliterated, and large portions of text rendered unreadable. The FBI's files, which were supposed to provide transparency about the secret operations conducted during COINTELPRO, remain riddled with gaps and silences. These redactions create a palpable sense of absence, a deliberate concealment of truth that leaves the reader grasping for meaning in what is left unsaid.

The redacted documents point to the power of ignorance and secrecy in the workings of the state. Information is controlled, hidden, and manipulated, creating a narrative that is incomplete at best and misleading at worst. These blacked-out spaces serve as a reminder that those in power control not only the present but also the past—by determining what is remembered and what is forgotten, what is revealed and what is concealed.

The emptiness in these files is not the liberating emptiness of Zen but a form of bureaucratic emptiness designed to obscure accountability. The lack of transparency serves the purpose of protecting those in power, shielding them from scrutiny and public oversight. It creates a barrier between the truth and the people who seek it, ensuring that the full extent of COINTELPRO's actions remains hidden from view.

The Power of Hidden Information

ZEN AND THE ART OF COINTELPRO

The redacted sections of the FBI files raise important questions about the nature of knowledge, secrecy, and power. In a surveillance state, the government often holds a monopoly on information, using it as a tool of control. The FBI's operations during COINTELPRO were built on the foundation of hidden information—surveillance, covert infiltration, and disinformation campaigns. The very nature of these operations depended on secrecy, and even decades later, the full truth of what happened remains elusive.

This creates a dynamic where power is maintained through the control of knowledge. Those who have access to information wield tremendous power over those who do not. COINTELPRO's success relied on its ability to gather information about the movements it sought to dismantle while keeping its own activities hidden from public view. The activists and leaders targeted by COINTELPRO were often unaware of the extent of the FBI's surveillance, infiltration, and manipulation until years later, when the redacted files were finally released.

Yet even when these files were made public, they were so heavily censored that much of the story remained hidden. The blacked-out sections serve as a metaphor for the ways in which power operates through the control of knowledge. By withholding information, the state creates a sense of uncertainty and confusion, making it difficult for the public to fully understand what happened, let alone hold those responsible accountable.

This dynamic of hidden information creates a profound sense of emptiness—an absence of truth that leaves us grappling with questions that may never be answered. What was said in those blacked-out sentences? Who were the individuals whose names were redacted? What actions were taken that remain concealed from public view? These gaps in the historical record remind us of the ways in which power operates not just through what is said, but through what is left unsaid.

What Can Be Known, and What Remains Unknowable

In Zen practice, one of the central teachings is the acceptance of uncertainty and the unknowable. The mind often craves certainty and control, seeking to understand everything and create a coherent narrative of reality. However, Zen teaches that this craving for certainty is itself a source of suffering. The nature of existence is fluid, dynamic, and constantly changing, and it is impossible to fully grasp or control it.

This teaching has profound implications for how we approach the empty spaces in the FBI files. The redacted sections create a sense of frustration and confusion, as they prevent us from knowing the full truth of what happened during COINTELPRO. But Zen invites us to approach this frustration with a different perspective. Rather than clinging to the desire for complete knowledge and certainty, Zen teaches us to embrace the mystery and uncertainty of life.

The emptiness in the FBI files reflects the inherent unknowability of the past. Even with all the information in the world, we can never fully understand the complexity of

ZEN AND THE ART OF COINTELPRO

historical events or the motivations of those involved. There will always be gaps, silences, and ambiguities. Zen teaches us to sit with this uncertainty, to accept the limitations of our knowledge, and to find peace in the midst of not knowing.

This does not mean that we should stop seeking the truth or abandon the pursuit of justice. On the contrary, Zen encourages us to engage fully with the world and to work for change. But it also reminds us that our efforts will always be limited by the complexity of reality and the impermanence of all things. The redacted FBI files serve as a reminder of the limitations of human knowledge, and Zen teaches us to approach these limitations with equanimity and acceptance.

The Nature of Truth in a World of Controlled Information

In a world where information is controlled and manipulated, the very concept of truth becomes elusive. The redacted FBI files illustrate how those in power can shape the narrative of history by controlling what is known and what is hidden. But Zen offers a different understanding of truth—one that is not dependent on external facts or information but arises from direct experience and inner clarity.

Zen teaches that truth is not something that can be grasped intellectually or controlled by external authorities. It is found in the present moment, in the direct experience of reality as it is. This type of truth is not about knowing all the facts or having access to all the information. It is about seeing clearly, without attachment or delusion, the nature of existence.

In the context of COINTELPRO and the FBI files, this Zen understanding of truth invites us to look beyond the redactions and the hidden information. While it is important to seek accountability and transparency, Zen reminds us that the ultimate truth lies not in the files themselves but in how we respond to the world around us. The emptiness in the files can be seen as a reflection of the emptiness of all things—the impermanence, uncertainty, and interconnectedness of reality.

By cultivating mindfulness and awareness, we can approach the unknown not with fear or frustration but with curiosity and openness. Zen teaches us to embrace the emptiness, to find wisdom in the spaces where information is withheld, and to recognize that even in the absence of full knowledge, we can still act with compassion and clarity.

Meditating on Emptiness: Lessons from the FBI Files

The redacted FBI files from the COINTELPRO era offer a unique opportunity to meditate on the nature of emptiness and truth. As we engage with these documents, we are confronted with the power of ignorance and secrecy—the ways in which information is controlled and hidden by those in power. But we are also invited to reflect on the Zen teachings of emptiness, impermanence, and the limitations of human knowledge.

What can these redacted documents teach us about the nature of truth? How can we navigate a world where information is often withheld or manipulated? And what does Zen have to

ZEN AND THE ART OF COINTELPRO

offer as we grapple with the emptiness left behind by the FBI's actions?

In the end, Zen teaches us that emptiness is not something to be feared or resisted. It is an essential aspect of existence, a reflection of the interconnected, ever-changing nature of reality. By embracing this emptiness, we can find peace in the midst of uncertainty and learn to act with wisdom and compassion, even when the full truth remains hidden from view.

Zazen in the Shadow of Big Brother

Zazen, the seated meditation at the core of Zen practice, is more than a method of cultivating mindfulness and awareness—it is a profound act of stillness and surrender. In a world increasingly defined by surveillance, coercion, and control, the simple act of sitting in meditation can serve as a quiet but radical form of resistance. By turning inward and seeking refuge in the present moment, Zazen offers an inner sanctuary that no external authority can reach, a space where freedom from the pressures of society is not only possible but essential.

This chapter looks into the power of Zazen in the context of modern surveillance, exploring how meditation can offer liberation from the psychological burdens imposed by constant observation. It will also provide practical guidance on how to incorporate mindfulness practices into daily life, helping readers to cultivate inner peace and clarity in a world where privacy is increasingly compromised.

In the shadow of Big Brother, where external forces constantly seek to monitor and manipulate our thoughts and behaviors, Zazen serves as a path to reclaim mental and emotional autonomy. Through the simple act of sitting still, practitioners can create an inner sanctuary that transcends the watchful eyes of the state, corporations, or social media algorithms. This chapter will explore how the practice of Zazen not only cultivates inner freedom but also becomes an act of rebellion against societal control.

ZEN AND THE ART OF COINTELPRO

Zazen as an Act of Stillness and Rebellion

Zazen, often translated as "seated meditation," is a fundamental practice in Zen Buddhism. It involves sitting in a specific posture—cross-legged, with hands placed in a cosmic mudra—and focusing on the breath or simply observing the mind. The practice is deceptively simple, yet it offers profound insights into the nature of existence. Through Zazen, practitioners learn to let go of thoughts, distractions, and attachments, and to rest in the awareness of the present moment.

In the context of a society that thrives on speed, distraction, and constant activity, the act of sitting still in meditation can feel countercultural, even rebellious. In Zazen, there is no productivity, no measurable outcome, no external validation. It is a practice of being rather than doing—a rejection of the capitalist notion that value is derived from constant output. This stillness, in and of itself, is an act of defiance against a world that demands perpetual motion.

Zazen is a return to simplicity, to the direct experience of the present moment. It is a practice that cultivates inner peace, but it also offers a quiet form of resistance to the external pressures that seek to dominate our lives. In the shadow of Big Brother—whether that be the government, corporations, or even the social media platforms that shape our perceptions—the ability to turn inward and find peace within ourselves becomes a radical act. It is a refusal to be controlled by the forces of surveillance and coercion that permeate modern life.

In this way, Zazen offers an antidote to the anxieties and fears that arise from living under constant surveillance. By sitting still and observing the flow of thoughts, sensations, and emotions, practitioners develop the capacity to see through the illusions created by fear and control. They come to realize that true freedom is not found in external circumstances but in the ability to remain centered and grounded in the midst of any situation.

Surveillance as a Form of Control

To understand the power of Zazen as a form of rebellion, it is important to first examine the role of surveillance in modern society. Surveillance, in its many forms, is a tool of control. Whether it is the government monitoring communications, corporations tracking our online behavior, or social media platforms collecting data on our preferences and interactions, the act of being watched shapes how we behave. Surveillance exerts a subtle but pervasive influence on our thoughts, decisions, and identities.

This form of control is often invisible, yet its effects are profound. The knowledge that we are being watched, even if only passively, creates a psychological pressure to conform. We may alter our behavior to fit social norms, avoid controversial opinions, or censor ourselves out of fear of repercussions. Over time, this surveillance-driven self-regulation becomes internalized, and we become our own monitors, perpetually assessing and adjusting our behavior to align with external expectations.

ZEN AND THE ART OF COINTELPRO

In this context, the practice of Zazen becomes an act of liberation. When we sit in meditation, we turn away from the external world and direct our attention inward. We are no longer performing for an audience, nor are we subject to the pressures of surveillance. In Zazen, there is no need to hide, conform, or present a curated version of ourselves. Instead, we allow ourselves to simply be—raw, unfiltered, and authentic.

Zazen creates a space where we can observe the patterns of thought and emotion that arise in response to external pressures, without being consumed by them. It allows us to witness the ways in which surveillance and control shape our sense of self, and to begin to disentangle ourselves from those influences. Through this practice, we cultivate the ability to remain centered and grounded, even in a world that seeks to control and manipulate us.

The Psychological Toll of Surveillance

Living in a surveillance society has far-reaching psychological consequences. The knowledge that we are being watched creates a constant low-level anxiety, a sense of being on guard. We become hyper-aware of how we are perceived, and this awareness shapes our behavior in subtle but significant ways. Over time, the pressure to conform to social norms, avoid controversy, and present a curated image of ourselves can erode our sense of authenticity and inner freedom.

Surveillance also fosters a sense of isolation. When we feel that our actions are being scrutinized, we may become hesitant to express ourselves fully or engage in meaningful connections with others. We may avoid controversial conversations or shy away from activism out of fear of being targeted or labeled. This isolation is compounded by the fact that surveillance is often invisible—we may not even be aware of who is watching us or why. This creates a sense of uncertainty and paranoia, further deepening the psychological toll.

In the face of these challenges, Zazen offers a powerful tool for reclaiming mental and emotional autonomy. The practice of meditation helps us to develop a sense of inner clarity and resilience, allowing us to navigate the pressures of surveillance without losing our sense of self. By turning inward and cultivating mindfulness, we create a refuge from the external world, a space where we can reconnect with our true nature and find peace amidst the chaos.

Zazen teaches us to observe the mind without attachment, to witness the flow of thoughts and emotions without being swept away by them. This skill is invaluable in a world where external forces constantly seek to shape our thoughts and behaviors. Through meditation, we develop the capacity to see through the illusions created by surveillance and control, and to remain grounded in our own inner truth.

Zazen as a Path to Inner Freedom

At its core, Zazen is a practice of liberation. It is not about escaping from the world or avoiding the challenges of life, but about finding freedom within ourselves, regardless of external circumstances. In a surveillance society, where our every move is potentially monitored and scrutinized, this inner freedom becomes all the more important.

Through Zazen, we learn to let go of the need for external validation and approval. We come to see that our sense of self is not dependent on how we are perceived by others, but on our own direct experience of the present moment. This realization is deeply empowering, as it allows us to navigate the pressures of surveillance with a sense of equanimity and peace.

The stillness of Zazen creates a space where we can reconnect with our true nature, free from the distortions imposed by surveillance and control. In this space, we are no longer defined by the expectations of society or the judgments of others. Instead, we are able to rest in the awareness of our own being, free from the need to perform or conform.

This inner freedom is not something that can be taken away by external forces. It is a state of mind that transcends the limitations of the physical world, allowing us to remain centered and grounded no matter what challenges we face. In this way, Zazen offers a path to liberation that is both deeply personal and profoundly transformative.

Practical Mindfulness in a Surveillance Society

Incorporating mindfulness practices into daily life can help us navigate the challenges of living in a surveillance society. While Zazen is the formal practice of seated meditation, mindfulness can be cultivated in any moment, regardless of what we are doing. By developing a habit of mindful awareness, we can create a sense of inner clarity and resilience that allows us to respond to the pressures of surveillance with equanimity and peace.

Here are some practical ways to incorporate mindfulness into your daily life as a form of resistance against societal control:

1. Mindful Breathing: One of the simplest and most effective ways to cultivate mindfulness is through mindful breathing. Take a few moments each day to focus on your breath, observing the sensations of inhaling and exhaling without trying to change or control them. This practice helps to anchor you in the present moment, creating a sense of inner stillness and clarity.

2. Mindful Observation: Throughout the day, take time to observe your thoughts, emotions, and behaviors with curiosity and non-judgment. Notice how the knowledge of being watched or monitored might influence your actions or decisions. By bringing awareness to these patterns, you can begin to disentangle yourself from the subtle pressures of surveillance.

3. Digital Detox: In a world where our online activities are constantly tracked and monitored, taking regular breaks from technology can be a powerful act of rebellion. Set aside time each day to disconnect from your devices and reconnect with the present moment. Use this time for meditation, walking in nature, or engaging in activities that nourish your mind and spirit.

4. Mindful Communication: In a surveillance society, the fear of being monitored can lead to self-censorship and isolation.

ZEN AND THE ART OF COINTELPRO

Practice mindful communication by engaging in honest, open conversations with others, even when it feels uncomfortable. By speaking your truth and listening with compassion, you can create deeper connections with others and resist the isolating effects of surveillance.

5. Cultivating Compassion: Surveillance thrives on fear and division. One of the most powerful ways to resist this is by cultivating compassion for yourself and others. Through mindfulness, practice extending kindness and understanding to those around you, even in the face of fear or uncertainty. Compassion is a force that can dissolve the boundaries created by surveillance, fostering a sense of connection and unity.

Inner Freedom in an Age of Control

Zazen, in its stillness and simplicity, offers a powerful path to inner freedom in a world increasingly defined by surveillance and control. By turning inward and cultivating mindfulness, we can create a sanctuary within ourselves, a space where external forces cannot reach. This inner sanctuary becomes a source of strength, resilience, and clarity, allowing us to navigate the pressures of a surveillance society with grace and equanimity.

In the shadow of Big Brother, Zazen offers more than just a practice of meditation—it offers a way of being that resists the forces of control and domination. Through mindfulness, we reclaim our mental and emotional autonomy, refusing to be shaped by the external pressures that seek to define us. In this way, Zazen becomes a path not only to personal liberation but also to collective empowerment, as we learn to cultivate peace and freedom in the midst of a world that seeks to control us.

In this chapter, we have explored how the practice of Zazen offers a form of resistance to the surveillance society, providing practical tools for incorporating mindfulness into daily life. As we continue to face the challenges of living in an increasingly controlled world, the teachings of Zen offer a timeless reminder that true freedom is found not in the external world, but in the stillness and clarity of our own minds. By embracing this truth, we can navigate the complexities of modern life with wisdom, compassion, and inner peace.

Disinformation as Delusion

In an age where information flows ceaselessly, distinguishing truth from falsehood becomes increasingly challenging. Disinformation, particularly as wielded by institutions like the FBI's COINTELPRO, serves as a tool of manipulation, designed to confuse, divide, and undermine social movements. These deliberate false narratives create chaos, fostering an environment where discernment is obscured, and clarity is lost. This chapter explores the parallels between the disinformation tactics employed by COINTELPRO and the Zen understanding of delusion as a fundamental barrier to enlightenment.

Understanding Disinformation

Disinformation is intentionally misleading information spread to influence public perception or behavior. COINTELPRO was infamous for its use of this tactic, employing techniques such as propaganda, infiltration, and psychological manipulation to disrupt political and social movements. By sowing discord and mistrust among activists, COINTELPRO effectively undermined the effectiveness of movements that sought social justice and systemic change.

One notable example of COINTELPRO's disinformation tactics involved the Black Panther Party (BPP). The FBI viewed the BPP as a significant threat and employed various strategies to discredit the organization. These included planting false stories in the media, promoting internal conflict among members, and spreading rumors about leadership. The goal was not merely to surveil but to create a narrative that would fracture the party from within, eroding public support and undermining its legitimacy.

Disinformation thrives in a society where trust in institutions has eroded. When citizens question the credibility of the media, the government, or even one another, it becomes easier for false narratives to take root. This distrust fuels a cycle of disinformation, making it difficult for individuals to discern truth from fiction.

The Zen Perspective on Delusio

In Zen Buddhism, delusion is regarded as one of the primary obstacles to enlightenment. It manifests as ignorance, misunderstanding, and the inability to see things as they truly are. Delusion clouds our perception, distorting our understanding of reality and preventing us from accessing deeper truths.

Delusion can take many forms, from self-deception to societal narratives that shape our beliefs and behaviors. In the realm of politics, delusion might manifest as adherence to false narratives or conspiracy theories, while personally, it might present as unexamined beliefs about oneself or others.

Zen teachings emphasize the importance of discernment, encouraging practitioners to investigate their thoughts and beliefs critically. By recognizing the ways in which delusion operates, individuals can cultivate greater clarity and insight, ultimately leading to a more profound understanding of themselves and the world around them.

Disinformation and the Path to Delusion

The spread of disinformation serves to create a landscape of confusion and mistrust, not only in the political sphere but also within our own minds. False narratives can seep into our consciousness, distorting our perceptions and shaping our understanding of reality. This distortion leads to delusion, obscuring the truth and making it difficult to discern what is genuine and what is manufactured.

The disinformation campaigns employed by COINTELPRO illustrate how external forces can manipulate public perception, but they also reveal how individuals can internalize these false narratives. The psychological toll of living in a world rife with disinformation can lead to anxiety, mistrust, and a sense of helplessness. When we are bombarded with conflicting information, it becomes challenging to discern what is true, leading to confusion and paralysis.

In a society where disinformation is prevalent, Zen practices can provide a pathway to clarity. Through mindfulness and self-reflection, individuals can cultivate discernment, learning to navigate the complexities of the information landscape with greater wisdom. Zen invites us to question our beliefs and assumptions, to investigate the narratives we consume, and to develop a deeper understanding of the nature of truth.

The Role of Mindfulness in Cultivating Discernment

STEVE SHORT

Mindfulness serves as a powerful tool in combating the effects of disinformation and delusion. By fostering awareness and presence, mindfulness allows us to engage with our thoughts and beliefs critically. This practice encourages us to observe our internal dialogue, question our assumptions, and examine the sources of the information we consume.

Mindfulness also helps us recognize when we are reacting to fear or anxiety, emotions that often drive us toward uncritical acceptance of false narratives. In moments of uncertainty, it is easy to cling to information that aligns with our fears or biases, reinforcing delusions rather than challenging them. Through mindfulness, we can cultivate the ability to pause, reflect, and choose our responses with greater clarity.

Incorporating mindfulness practices into our daily lives can take many forms, from formal meditation to informal moments of awareness. Here are a few practical ways to cultivate mindfulness and discernment:

1. Mindful Consumption of Information: Before accepting information as truth, take a moment to pause and reflect. Consider the source of the information, its context, and the potential motivations behind it. By practicing mindful consumption, we can begin to filter out disinformation and discern the validity of what we encounter.

2. Journaling and Self-Reflection: Writing can be a powerful tool for cultivating self-awareness and clarity. Regularly reflecting on our thoughts, beliefs, and emotional responses can help us identify patterns of delusion and misinformation.

ZEN AND THE ART OF COINTELPRO

Journaling allows us to externalize our thoughts, making it easier to examine and challenge them.

3. Engaging in Open Dialogue: Discussing ideas and beliefs with others can provide new perspectives and insights. Seek out conversations with those who hold differing viewpoints, approaching discussions with curiosity rather than defensiveness. Open dialogue encourages us to question our assumptions and consider alternative narratives.

4. Practicing Non-Attachment: Zen teachings emphasize the importance of non-attachment, particularly to beliefs and opinions. Recognizing that our thoughts are not inherently true allows us to approach information with a sense of openness and curiosity. By letting go of the need to be right, we create space for discernment and understanding.

5. Meditative Inquiry: Incorporating inquiry into your meditation practice can deepen your understanding of delusion and disinformation. Ask yourself questions such as: What beliefs am I holding onto? How do these beliefs shape my perception of reality? What is the source of my information? By exploring these questions with curiosity, you can cultivate greater clarity.

Disinformation and the Collective Consciousness

Disinformation does not only affect individuals; it shapes the collective consciousness of society. False narratives can create divisions, perpetuate stereotypes, and foster an environment of distrust. When disinformation permeates the public sphere, it becomes challenging for individuals to come together in pursuit of shared goals or understanding.

The tactics employed by COINTELPRO serve as a reminder of how powerful disinformation can be in fracturing movements. By spreading rumors, fostering division, and manipulating public perception, COINTELPRO effectively undermined social movements that sought justice and equality. The repercussions of these tactics continue to resonate today, as societal divisions deepen and mistrust grows.

Zen teachings emphasize the interconnectedness of all beings, highlighting the importance of compassion and understanding. In the face of disinformation, it becomes essential to cultivate empathy and seek common ground. By fostering connections and engaging in open dialogue, we can begin to dismantle the divisions created by false narratives.

The Journey Toward Clarity

The journey toward clarity is an ongoing process, one that requires continuous self-reflection and inquiry. Disinformation and delusion are pervasive, and the impact of these forces can be profound. However, through mindfulness and discernment, individuals can cultivate greater awareness and understanding, allowing them to navigate the complexities of the world with wisdom.

Recognizing the ways in which disinformation operates empowers us to take responsibility for our beliefs and perceptions. By questioning the narratives we consume and examining the motivations behind them, we can begin to free ourselves from the chains of delusion. This journey toward clarity is not merely an intellectual exercise; it is a spiritual practice that invites us to deepen our understanding of ourselves and the world.

Zen Practices for Cultivating Clarity

As we navigate the landscape of disinformation and delusion, the following Zen practices can support our journey toward clarity:

1. Zazen (Seated Meditation): Regular Zazen practice fosters inner stillness and awareness, creating a foundation for clarity. During meditation, observe the flow of thoughts without attachment, allowing yourself to become aware of any delusions or misconceptions that arise. This practice helps cultivate discernment, enabling you to navigate the complexities of information with greater ease.

2. Walking Meditation: Walking meditation combines movement with mindfulness, allowing you to engage with the present moment while reflecting on your surroundings. As you walk, focus on each step, bringing awareness to your breath and the sensations in your body. This practice encourages grounding and presence, helping you cultivate clarity in your thoughts.

3. Mindful Listening: In conversations, practice active listening without formulating your response while the other person speaks. This practice allows you to fully engage with their perspective, fostering empathy and understanding. By approaching discussions with an open heart and mind, you can challenge your own beliefs and deepen your understanding of differing viewpoints.

4. Contemplative Reading: Engage with texts that challenge your beliefs and assumptions. Approach reading as a contemplative practice, allowing yourself to reflect deeply on the ideas presented. Take notes, highlight passages that resonate with you, and engage in self-inquiry about how the material influences your understanding.

5. Community Engagement: Seek opportunities to engage with others in discussions about disinformation and societal issues. Participate in community dialogues, workshops, or study groups that focus on critical thinking and discernment. Building connections with others can foster a sense of collective responsibility and promote clarity in navigating complex issues.

Embracing Uncertainty

In a world rife with disinformation, embracing uncertainty is an essential aspect of cultivating clarity. We may not always have access to the truth, and navigating the complexities of information can feel overwhelming. However, by approaching uncertainty with curiosity and openness, we can cultivate resilience and adaptability.

Zen teachings emphasize the importance of accepting impermanence and uncertainty as fundamental aspects of existence. Rather than clinging to fixed beliefs or narratives, we can cultivate a sense of flexibility, allowing our understanding to evolve as we gain new insights. Embracing uncertainty encourages us to remain open to new perspectives and possibilities, ultimately leading to greater clarity.

The Path to Enlightenment Through Discernment

Disinformation serves as a profound barrier to enlightenment, creating delusions that obscure our understanding of truth. However, through mindfulness, self-reflection, and discernment, we can navigate the complexities of information with greater clarity. By recognizing the tactics of disinformation and embracing Zen principles, we can cultivate a deeper understanding of ourselves and the world around us.

The journey toward clarity is ongoing, requiring continuous inquiry and engagement. As we confront the disinformation that permeates our lives, we must remember that the path to enlightenment begins within. By cultivating awareness, compassion, and discernment, we can dismantle the barriers of delusion and open ourselves to the deeper truths that lie beyond.

As we continue to explore the themes of Zen and the realities of COINTELPRO, we invite readers to reflect on their own beliefs and narratives. In a world rife with disinformation, the quest for truth is a collective journey, one that requires the courage to question, the humility to listen, and the wisdom to discern. Through mindfulness and self-awareness, we can navigate the complexities of our lives with clarity, compassion, and a commitment to uncovering the truth.

Surveillance Capitalism and the New COINTELPRO

The legacy of COINTELPRO (Counter Intelligence Program) may have officially ended in the 1970s, but its tactics and philosophies have taken on a new life in the era of surveillance capitalism. This chapter explores the connections between COINTELPRO's covert operations and contemporary practices of data mining, social media manipulation, and the pervasive surveillance conducted by both corporate and state entities. As we delve into these topics, we will confront the pressing question: How can we live mindfully and freely in an age where our personal information serves as the new currency of control?

The Evolution of COINTELPRO

Before examining the modern landscape of surveillance capitalism, it's important to understand COINTELPRO's origins and objectives. Established in the late 1950s, COINTELPRO was designed to infiltrate and disrupt civil rights organizations, leftist groups, and any entities perceived as threats to national security. Through a range of tactics—including infiltration, disinformation, and psychological manipulation—the FBI sought to control and undermine these movements.

COINTELPRO's impact was significant; it instigated paranoia, division, and mistrust among activists, leading to fractured movements and individual trauma. Although the program was officially disbanded in 1971, its legacy endures in the methods employed by modern institutions to surveil, manipulate, and control individuals and groups.

Surveillance Capitalism: The New Frontier

The term "surveillance capitalism," coined by Shoshana Zuboff, refers to the commodification of personal data by corporations and the use of this data to predict and influence human behavior. In a world increasingly driven by technology, our online activities generate a wealth of information that is harvested, analyzed, and monetized.

Unlike traditional capitalism, which is primarily concerned with goods and services, surveillance capitalism is rooted in the manipulation of behavior. Companies collect data on consumers, allowing them to create predictive models that not only inform their marketing strategies but also shape user experiences and preferences. The goal is to generate profit by controlling consumer behavior and ensuring that users remain engaged with their platforms.

Data Mining and Social Media Manipulation

At the heart of surveillance capitalism is data mining—the process of extracting valuable insights from large datasets. Social media platforms, in particular, have become key players in this arena, using sophisticated algorithms to collect and analyze user data.

Consider platforms like Facebook and Instagram, which track user interactions, preferences, and behaviors to create highly targeted advertisements. The algorithms employed by these platforms not only dictate what content users see but also manipulate their emotional responses and opinions. This manipulation raises ethical questions about the extent to which these platforms influence individual autonomy and decision-making.

One of the most alarming aspects of social media manipulation is its potential to create echo chambers, environments where individuals are only exposed to information that reinforces their existing beliefs. This phenomenon can amplify divisions within society, polarizing opinions and contributing to the erosion of trust. The tactics used to create and sustain these echo chambers echo the methods employed by COINTELPRO to sow discord among activists, undermining movements from within.

The Omnipresence of Corporate and State Surveillance

The rise of surveillance capitalism has been accompanied by an increase in both corporate and state surveillance. Governments around the world have adopted technologies that enable mass surveillance of their citizens, often justified by claims of national security or public safety. This surveillance takes many forms, from CCTV cameras in public spaces to the monitoring of online activities through data collection and analysis.

In the United States, the legacy of COINTELPRO has not only influenced governmental approaches to surveillance but has also contributed to a culture of fear and mistrust. The events of September 11, 2001, led to the implementation of the USA PATRIOT Act, which expanded the government's surveillance capabilities and diminished civil liberties. The state's interest in monitoring dissent and social movements persists, with organizations like the FBI continuing to surveil activist groups under the guise of national security.

The relationship between corporate and state surveillance is symbiotic. Corporations collect vast amounts of data on consumers, which can then be shared with government entities for various purposes, including intelligence gathering. This collaboration raises important questions about the implications of surveillance capitalism for democracy and individual freedom.

The Ethics of Data Collection and Privacy

As surveillance capitalism continues to evolve, ethical concerns surrounding data collection and privacy have become increasingly pressing. The commodification of personal information raises fundamental questions about consent, autonomy, and the right to privacy. In an age where our online actions are meticulously tracked, individuals often find themselves navigating a complex web of surveillance with limited awareness of the implications.

The concept of informed consent has become murky in the digital realm. When users sign up for social media platforms or online services, they often agree to lengthy terms and conditions that few read in detail. These agreements frequently include clauses that grant companies extensive rights to collect, analyze, and share user data, often without transparent disclosure of how this data will be used.

Moreover, individuals may feel powerless to challenge or understand the algorithms that govern their online experiences. This power imbalance mirrors the tactics used by COINTELPRO, where individuals found themselves manipulated and surveilled without their knowledge. In both cases, a lack of transparency and accountability contributes to a sense of disempowerment.

Living Mindfully in a Surveillance Society

In the face of pervasive surveillance, how can individuals cultivate mindfulness and autonomy? The principles of Zen philosophy offer valuable insights into navigating the complexities of living in a surveillance society. Here are some ways to apply these principles:

1. Cultivating Awareness of Digital Footprints

One of the first steps to living mindfully in a surveillance society is developing an awareness of one's digital footprints. This involves recognizing that every online action leaves a trace—be it a social media post, a purchase, or a search query. By acknowledging the permanence of these footprints, individuals can make more intentional choices about their online behaviors.

To cultivate this awareness, consider the following practices:

- **Reflect on Online Interactions:** Before posting or sharing information online, take a moment to consider the potential impact. How might this information be interpreted? Who might have access to it?

- Practice Digital Minimalism: Evaluate your online presence and consider simplifying your digital interactions. Reducing the number of platforms you engage with can help minimize your exposure to surveillance and create space for more meaningful connections.

- Set Boundaries: Determine what personal information you are comfortable sharing online. Be intentional about privacy settings and consider the potential consequences of disclosing sensitive information.

2. Embracing Critical Thinking and Media Literacy

In a world filled with misinformation and manipulation, cultivating critical thinking skills and media literacy is essential. This involves questioning the sources of information we consume and recognizing the biases inherent in various narratives.

To foster critical thinking:

- Seek Diverse Perspectives: Engage with sources that present differing viewpoints, and approach information with curiosity rather than defensiveness. This practice encourages a broader understanding of complex issues.

- Fact-Check Information: Before sharing or acting on information, verify its accuracy. Utilize fact-checking websites and reputable news sources to assess the validity of claims.

- **Participate in Discussions:** Engage in conversations about current events and social issues with friends, family, or community members. Open dialogue encourages critical thinking and helps individuals challenge their assumptions.

3. Engaging in Collective Action

The tactics of COINTELPRO were designed to fracture movements and sow discord among activists. In contrast, collective action can serve as a powerful antidote to the isolating effects of surveillance capitalism. By coming together to advocate for privacy rights, data protection, and digital freedoms, individuals can reclaim agency in the face of systemic control.

Consider the following ways to engage in collective action:

- **Join Advocacy Groups:** Align yourself with organizations that work to protect civil liberties and privacy rights in the digital age. Engaging with these groups can amplify your voice and contribute to meaningful change.

- **Participate in Community Dialogues:** Attend local forums, workshops, or town halls focused on digital rights and surveillance issues. Community engagement fosters awareness and encourages collective action.

- **Support Legislation for Data Protection:** Stay informed about legislation related to data privacy and surveillance, and advocate for policies that protect individual rights and promote transparency.

Zen and the Art of Resilience

ZEN AND THE ART OF COINTELPRO

Zen philosophy teaches that resilience emerges from acceptance of impermanence and the cultivation of inner peace. In the context of surveillance capitalism, this resilience can manifest as a commitment to mindfulness, critical thinking, and ethical engagement with the digital world.

1. Embracing Impermanence

Recognizing that all things are impermanent allows individuals to detach from their identities as digital consumers. By cultivating a mindset of non-attachment, we can navigate the complexities of digital life with greater ease. This practice involves:

- **Releasing the Need for Validation:** Social media often fosters a culture of comparison and validation. Embrace the idea that your self-worth is not defined by online metrics, such as likes or followers.

- **Practicing Detachment:** Approach online interactions with a sense of detachment. Recognize that you are not your digital persona, and allow yourself to step back from the pressures of constant connectivity.

2. Finding Peace Amidst Chaos

In the face of overwhelming information and manipulation, finding moments of peace becomes essential. Mindfulness practices can provide individuals with the tools to cultivate stillness amidst chaos.

- **Incorporate Mindfulness into Daily Life:** Practice mindfulness throughout your day, whether through formal meditation, mindful walking, or simply taking a moment to breathe deeply. These practices can create a sense of calm and clarity.

- **Create a Digital Detox:** Periodically disconnect from digital devices to engage in activities that foster presence and connection with the physical world. Nature walks, reading, or spending time with loved ones can recharge your mental and emotional well-being.

Navigating the New COINTELPRO

The legacy of COINTELPRO lives on in the digital age, as surveillance capitalism employs tactics reminiscent of those used by the FBI to control and manipulate individuals and movements. However, by embracing mindfulness, cultivating awareness, and engaging in collective action, individuals can navigate the complexities of surveillance with resilience and clarity.

Living mindfully in a surveillance society requires continuous self-reflection and engagement with the broader community. As we confront the challenges posed by data mining, social media manipulation, and pervasive surveillance, we must remember that our personal information is not merely a commodity but a reflection of our humanity.

Through the lens of Zen philosophy, we can find strength in the face of uncertainty, embracing the impermanence of existence while seeking truth, compassion, and connection. By reclaiming our agency and advocating for our rights in the digital realm, we can work towards a future that honors

ZEN AND THE ART OF COINTELPRO

individual autonomy and upholds the principles of freedom and dignity.

In this journey toward mindfulness, let us remember that we are not alone. Together, we can challenge the structures of surveillance capitalism and forge a path toward a more equitable and compassionate world.

The Mirror of the State

In the intricate dance between government and society, the state acts as a mirror—a distorted reflection of the collective psyche. Through the lens of Zen philosophy, we explore this notion, examining how the state projects fear, division, and control back onto its citizens. The FBI's COINTELPRO program serves as a compelling case study, revealing how the government mirrors societal anxieties and magnifies them through covert operations. In stark contrast, Zen teaches us that the mind, when clear and undisturbed, can reflect a deeper truth than any government apparatus, illuminating the path toward authenticity and liberation.

The State as a Distorted Mirror

The metaphor of the state as a mirror suggests that governments reflect the values, fears, and aspirations of their citizens. However, this reflection is not always accurate; it is often distorted by bias, propaganda, and a desire for control. In a society rife with conflict, inequality, and uncertainty, the state may exaggerate these issues, projecting a sense of threat that justifies oppressive measures. This distortion creates a feedback loop where the state's actions exacerbate societal fears, leading to further mistrust and division.

The Dynamics of Fear

Fear is a powerful force that can shape behavior, attitudes, and policies. When individuals feel threatened, they often seek safety and security, even if it comes at the cost of personal freedoms. The state exploits this vulnerability, magnifying societal fears to justify surveillance, censorship, and repression.

COINTELPRO exemplifies this dynamic. Initiated during a period of social upheaval in the 1960s, COINTELPRO sought to quell dissent by infiltrating and disrupting civil rights organizations, anti-war movements, and leftist groups. The FBI's portrayal of these movements as dangerous and subversive fed into a broader narrative of fear, reinforcing the perception that social change was a threat to national security.

This use of fear as a political tool is not unique to COINTELPRO; it is a recurring theme in statecraft throughout history. By projecting societal anxieties onto targeted groups, the government can rationalize actions that undermine civil liberties and suppress dissent. The state becomes a distorted mirror, reflecting back the fears it itself has amplified.

The Role of Propaganda

In addition to fear, propaganda plays a crucial role in shaping the state's narrative. Governments utilize propaganda to create a specific image of reality, influencing public perception and opinion. This manufactured reality can distort the truth, leading citizens to accept misinformation and relinquish critical thinking.

Throughout the COINTELPRO era, the FBI employed various propaganda techniques to demonize social movements. By labeling activists as "subversives" or "extremists," the government sought to delegitimize their struggles and stifle dissent. This manipulation of public perception is reminiscent of the way propaganda has been used throughout history to justify state violence and repression.

The state's ability to control the narrative is particularly potent in the digital age, where information spreads rapidly and misinformation can proliferate. Social media platforms serve as battlegrounds for competing narratives, further complicating the relationship between truth and perception. As citizens navigate this landscape, they must confront the challenges of discerning fact from fiction and resisting the allure of distorted reflections.

COINTELPRO as a Case Study

COINTELPRO provides a poignant illustration of how the state acts as a distorted mirror, reflecting and amplifying societal anxieties. Initially established to combat the perceived threat of communism, COINTELPRO's focus quickly shifted to suppressing civil rights movements and other grassroots organizations that sought social change.

The Targeting of Activists

The tactics employed by COINTELPRO included surveillance, infiltration, disinformation campaigns, and psychological warfare. Activists were often portrayed as dangerous radicals, and their movements were subjected to intense scrutiny. This targeting created an atmosphere of fear and mistrust within social movements, as individuals became wary of potential informants and government infiltration.

ZEN AND THE ART OF COINTELPRO

The impact of COINTELPRO was profound. Many activists experienced paranoia, anxiety, and distrust as a result of the government's covert operations. This psychological toll served to fragment movements and undermine collective action, further perpetuating the state's control over dissenting voices.

In examining COINTELPRO, we can see how the state's distorted mirror magnified societal fears of instability and change. By projecting these fears onto activists, the government justified its repressive measures and created a narrative that framed dissent as a threat to national security.

The Zen Perspective: A Clear Mirror

In contrast to the state's distorted mirror, Zen philosophy offers the image of a clear, undisturbed mind as a mirror of reality. When the mind is free from attachments, biases, and fears, it can reflect the world as it is—an unvarnished truth that transcends propaganda and manipulation.

The Practice of Mindfulness

Mindfulness is a central tenet of Zen practice, emphasizing the importance of present-moment awareness. Through mindfulness, individuals learn to observe their thoughts and emotions without judgment, cultivating a deeper understanding of their internal landscapes. This clarity of mind allows for a more accurate perception of reality, free from the distortions imposed by external forces.

In a society characterized by surveillance and manipulation, mindfulness becomes a powerful antidote to the state's projections. By cultivating awareness, individuals can break free from the patterns of fear and mistrust that the state seeks to instill. Mindfulness practices can help individuals reclaim agency over their perceptions, allowing them to see through the distortions of the state's mirror.

Embracing Non-Attachment

Another key aspect of Zen philosophy is the concept of non-attachment. When we cling to fixed beliefs or narratives, we limit our ability to see the world clearly. In a surveillance society, where information is often manipulated, non-attachment becomes essential for discerning truth from falsehood.

Non-attachment encourages individuals to approach information with curiosity rather than defensiveness. Instead of accepting the state's narrative at face value, individuals can cultivate a mindset of inquiry, questioning the motives behind the information they receive. This practice fosters critical thinking and empowers individuals to seek deeper truths beyond the surface.

Reclaiming Agency: A Call to Action

As we explore the relationship between the state and society, it is crucial to recognize that individuals have the power to reshape their realities. By cultivating a clear and undisturbed mind, we can challenge the distortions of the state's mirror and reclaim agency over our perceptions and actions.

1. Building Community

ZEN AND THE ART OF COINTELPRO

One of the most effective ways to counter the state's projections is to build strong, supportive communities. By coming together with others who share similar values and concerns, individuals can create spaces for open dialogue and collective action. Community engagement fosters trust, understanding, and resilience, enabling individuals to confront the state's distortions together.

- Participate in Local Activism: Engaging with local activist groups allows individuals to connect with like-minded individuals and work toward common goals. Collective action amplifies voices and challenges oppressive narratives.

- Create Safe Spaces for Dialogue: Establishing forums for open discussions encourages individuals to share their experiences, insights, and concerns. These spaces can foster understanding and solidarity, helping to counteract the divisive tactics of the state.

2. Advocating for Transparency and Accountability

In a world where government narratives can be distorted, advocating for transparency and accountability becomes paramount. Citizens must hold their governments accountable for their actions and demand clarity in the information presented to the public.

- Support Whistleblower Protections: Whistleblowers play a crucial role in exposing government misconduct and holding authorities accountable. Supporting protections for whistleblowers encourages individuals to speak out against injustices.

- **Engage with Civic Organizations:** Collaborating with organizations that promote transparency and government accountability can amplify efforts to challenge oppressive practices. Engaging with civic initiatives fosters a sense of empowerment and collective action.

3. Embracing Personal Reflection

Individual reflection is essential for cultivating a clear mind. By engaging in practices that promote self-awareness and mindfulness, individuals can develop a deeper understanding of their beliefs, biases, and motivations.

- **Incorporate Meditation into Daily Life:** Establishing a regular meditation practice allows individuals to cultivate mindfulness and clarity. Through meditation, one can observe thoughts and emotions without attachment, leading to greater self-awareness.

- **Reflect on Personal Narratives:** Take time to examine the narratives you hold about yourself and the world around you. Consider how these narratives may be influenced by external forces and whether they align with your authentic values.

Toward a Clearer Reflection

As we navigate the complexities of living in a society shaped by surveillance and manipulation, it is vital to recognize the power of the mind as a mirror. The state may project distorted reflections of fear and division, but through the principles of Zen, we can cultivate a clear and undisturbed mind that reflects deeper truths.

ZEN AND THE ART OF COINTELPRO

By embracing mindfulness, non-attachment, and community engagement, individuals can reclaim agency over their perceptions and challenge the narratives imposed by the state. In doing so, we illuminate a path toward authenticity and liberation, fostering a society where truth prevails over distortion.

The journey toward clarity is ongoing, requiring continuous self-reflection and engagement with the broader community. As we confront the challenges posed by the state's distorted mirror, let us remember that we possess the power to shape our realities. Through mindfulness and collective action, we can create a clearer reflection of ourselves and the world, one that honors our shared humanity and the pursuit of justice.

Compassion for the Oppressor

Zen, at its heart, teaches a profound and challenging truth: compassion must extend to all beings, even to those who cause harm. This tenet pushes the boundaries of empathy and moral understanding, asking us to cultivate compassion not just for the oppressed but also for the oppressors. In the context of COINTELPRO, this call is particularly difficult to embrace. How can we extend compassion to the architects of a program that caused so much damage, undermining social movements and devastating countless lives? How do we reconcile the need for justice with the need for empathy?

This chapter explores these difficult questions, drawing on Zen philosophy to guide the reader through the complexities of compassion in the face of systemic violence. It challenges the conventional dichotomy of victim and oppressor, offering an alternative lens through which to view power, responsibility, and the shared suffering that arises from the systems of oppression. Through this exploration, we begin to see that healing—both personal and societal—cannot be fully realized without addressing the humanity of those who wield power destructively.

Understanding the Oppressor: A Human Being Caught in Delusion

In Zen, the concept of delusion is central to understanding human suffering. Delusion, in this sense, refers to the misperceptions and misunderstandings that cloud our minds, causing us to act in ways that create suffering for ourselves and others. When we operate from a place of ignorance—whether it be ignorance of our own motivations, the suffering of others, or the interdependent nature of existence—we perpetuate harm. This applies not only to individuals but also to institutions and systems of power.

COINTELPRO, as an operation designed to suppress dissent, was built on a foundation of fear, ignorance, and delusion. The FBI, and the individuals who directed COINTELPRO, operated under the belief that social movements like the Civil Rights Movement, the Black Panther Party, and anti-Vietnam War groups posed existential threats to the stability of the nation. This belief, rooted in fear and a desire to maintain control, led to the justification of tactics that were harmful and oppressive.

Yet, in Zen, we are taught to see even these harmful actions as arising from a place of delusion. The oppressor, in this view, is not a one-dimensional figure of evil but a person caught in their own suffering, unaware of the harm they are inflicting or how deeply interconnected their actions are with the suffering of others. This perspective does not excuse or absolve wrongdoing; rather, it invites us to see the oppressor's humanity and the ways in which they, too, are victims of their own ignorance.

The Roots of Fear and Control

The need for control is often driven by fear. In the case of COINTELPRO, fear of social change, fear of losing power, and fear of the unknown fueled the program's operations. The individuals behind COINTELPRO believed they were protecting the country from chaos and instability. This fear distorted their perception of reality, leading them to view movements for justice and equality as threats rather than opportunities for societal growth.

From a Zen perspective, this clinging to control is itself a form of suffering. The more we try to grasp at power, the more we are driven by fear of losing it, and the less we are able to see the world clearly. In this sense, the architects of COINTELPRO were trapped in their own suffering, perpetuating violence as a means of trying to protect themselves from imagined threats. This delusion created a cycle of harm, with the oppressors causing suffering for others while deepening their own attachment to fear and control.

To extend compassion to these individuals is to recognize their suffering, even as we hold them accountable for the harm they caused. It is to understand that their actions, however destructive, were rooted in fear and ignorance, and that they too are deserving of the opportunity to awaken from this delusion.

Compassion Without Absolving Harm

Compassion, in Zen, is not about absolving harm or ignoring injustice. It is about seeing clearly the conditions that give rise to suffering and responding with wisdom and empathy. When we talk about cultivating compassion for the oppressor, we are not suggesting that we turn a blind eye to the harm they have caused. Instead, we are acknowledging that the oppressor, too, is caught in a web of suffering, and that true healing must involve addressing the suffering on both sides.

Accountability and Compassion

Accountability is a crucial aspect of justice. Those who wield power destructively must be held accountable for their actions. This is especially true in the case of COINTELPRO, where the government's covert operations caused lasting harm to individuals and movements fighting for justice. However, accountability does not preclude compassion.

In Zen, there is an understanding that people's actions arise from causes and conditions. These causes and conditions—fear, ignorance, greed, attachment to power—shape how individuals behave, particularly when they are placed in positions of authority. While it is essential to hold individuals accountable for the harm they cause, it is also possible to see that their actions are often the result of delusion and fear, rather than inherent malice.

This is where compassion comes in. Compassion for the oppressor means recognizing the suffering that drives their harmful actions while still advocating for justice and accountability. It means understanding that punishment alone will not break the cycle of suffering; only through addressing the root causes of oppression—fear, ignorance, and attachment to power—can we begin to heal both the oppressors and the oppressed.

Forgiveness as a Path to Liberation

In Zen, forgiveness is not a passive act of letting go but an active practice of liberation. When we hold on to anger, resentment, or hatred toward those who have harmed us, we keep ourselves trapped in a cycle of suffering. By practicing forgiveness—not in the sense of excusing harm, but in the sense of releasing our attachment to the pain—we free ourselves from the grip of anger and open the door to healing.

Forgiveness, in this sense, is not about condoning the actions of the oppressor. It is about recognizing that holding on to hatred only perpetuates suffering. By forgiving, we liberate ourselves from the emotional and psychological burden of resentment, allowing us to move forward with clarity and compassion.

In the case of COINTELPRO, this means acknowledging the deep harm caused by the program while also working toward healing. It means understanding that the individuals behind COINTELPRO were acting from a place of fear and delusion, and that true liberation for all involved requires breaking the cycle of fear and violence. Forgiveness, in this context, becomes a path to liberation—for the oppressed and the oppressor alike.

Beyond the Dichotomy of Victim and Oppressor

One of the most powerful teachings in Zen is the dissolution of dualities. The world is not divided into neat categories of good and evil, victim and oppressor. Instead, Zen teaches us to see the interconnectedness of all beings, the ways in which we are all part of a larger web of existence. This perspective challenges the conventional dichotomy of victim and oppressor, inviting us to see beyond the surface-level distinctions and recognize the shared humanity in all.

The Interconnectedness of Suffering

In Zen, suffering is understood as a universal condition. All beings, to some extent, experience suffering, whether through attachment, fear, or ignorance. This suffering is not isolated; it is interconnected. The suffering of the oppressed and the oppressor are linked, each feeding into the other in a cycle of harm.

When we view the world through this lens of interconnected suffering, the dichotomy between victim and oppressor begins to blur. The oppressor is not an isolated figure of power but someone who is also caught in the cycle of suffering, albeit in a different way. Their actions, while harmful, are driven by the same underlying causes that lead to suffering in all beings—fear, ignorance, attachment.

This understanding does not erase the need for justice. It does, however, open the possibility for a more compassionate response, one that seeks to heal the root causes of suffering rather than simply punish the outward manifestations. By recognizing the interconnectedness of suffering, we can begin to see that true healing requires addressing the suffering of both the oppressed and the oppressor.

Breaking the Cycle of Violence

The cycle of violence perpetuated by systems of oppression is one of the most destructive forces in society. It creates a feedback loop in which harm begets more harm, and suffering deepens on both sides. Breaking this cycle requires a fundamental shift in how we view power, control, and responsibility.

In Zen, breaking the cycle of violence begins with mindfulness and awareness. When we are mindful of our thoughts, emotions, and actions, we can begin to see the ways in which we are contributing to the cycle of suffering. This awareness allows us to make more conscious choices, responding to harm with compassion rather than perpetuating further violence.

For those in positions of power, breaking the cycle of violence means recognizing the ways in which fear and attachment to control drive harmful actions. It requires a willingness to confront the delusions that underlie oppressive systems and to cultivate compassion for those who have been harmed. This is not an easy path, but it is essential for creating a more just and compassionate society.

Compassion as a Radical Act

In a world where power is often wielded destructively, compassion can be a radical act. It challenges the conventional wisdom that might and control are the paths to safety and security, offering instead a vision of a world rooted in empathy and understanding. Compassion, in this sense, is not weakness; it is strength. It is the strength to see beyond fear and division, to recognize the shared humanity in all beings, and to work toward healing for both the oppressed and the oppressor.

Cultivating Compassion in Practice

ZEN AND THE ART OF COINTELPRO

Cultivating compassion for the oppressor is not a passive process; it requires active practice. In Zen, this practice often begins with self-compassion. By learning to be kind and understanding toward ourselves, we can begin to extend that compassion to others, even those who have caused harm.

- **Mindfulness Meditation:** Mindfulness meditation is a foundational practice in Zen that helps cultivate awareness and compassion. By sitting in stillness and observing our thoughts and emotions without judgment, we can begin to develop a deeper understanding of our own suffering and the suffering of others.

- **Loving-Kindness Meditation (Metta):** Another powerful practice for cultivating compassion is loving-kindness meditation, or Metta. In this practice, we focus on sending thoughts of love and compassion to ourselves, our loved ones, and eventually, even those who have harmed us. This practice helps soften the barriers of resentment and hatred, allowing us to approach others with empathy.

- **Engaging with Oppression Mindfully:** In the face of systemic oppression, it can be difficult to extend compassion to those in power. However, by approaching these situations with mindfulness, we can begin to see the fear and delusion that drive oppressive actions. This awareness allows us to respond with both compassion and a commitment to justice.

A Path Toward Collective Healing

Compassion for the oppressor is not an easy path, but it is a necessary one if we are to break the cycles of violence and suffering that perpetuate oppression. Zen teaches us that true compassion must extend to all beings, even those who cause harm. This does not mean ignoring or excusing injustice; it means recognizing the shared suffering that arises from systems of violence and working toward healing on all sides.

By cultivating compassion for the oppressor, we open the possibility for collective healing. We move beyond the dichotomy of victim and oppressor, recognizing the interconnectedness of suffering and the need for accountability, justice, and empathy. In doing so, we create the conditions for a more just and compassionate world, where all beings can find liberation from suffering.

The journey toward compassion is ongoing, requiring continuous practice and reflection. As we navigate the complexities of power and oppression, let us remember that the path to healing begins with understanding—both of ourselves and of those who wield power. Through mindfulness, compassion, and a commitment to justice, we can break the cycles of suffering and create a world where empathy and understanding guide our actions.

Waking Up in the Panopticon

Jeremy Bentham's concept of the Panopticon, a theoretical prison where inmates are always visible to the watchman but never sure when they are being observed, has long been regarded as a potent metaphor for the psychological effects of surveillance. Inmates, under the assumption that they could be observed at any moment, begin to self-regulate their behavior, internalizing the control mechanisms even when no one is watching. This structure was intended as a way to maintain order with minimal resources, ensuring that the mere *possibility* of surveillance would discipline those under observation.

In the modern world, the Panopticon extends far beyond Bentham's 18th-century prison. It has become a powerful symbol of the surveillance state—where citizens, much like Bentham's prisoners, live under the constant potential of being watched. Whether through government agencies, corporate data collection, or social media platforms, surveillance has permeated nearly every aspect of contemporary life. The lines between observer and observed, freedom and control, have blurred, leaving individuals to navigate a world in which the unseen gaze shapes their behavior, thoughts, and perceptions of reality.

This chapter explores the psychological effects of living in such a surveillance society, drawing parallels between Bentham's Panopticon and the mechanisms employed by COINTELPRO. It also examines how Zen practice can serve as a means of "waking up" from the illusion of constant surveillance, reclaiming inner freedom, and resisting the psychological grip of the Panopticon.

The Panopticon: A Metaphor for Modern Surveillance

Jeremy Bentham's Panopticon was a radical departure from traditional ideas of control and punishment. Instead of relying on brute force or physical restraint to maintain order, the Panopticon leveraged psychological control. Inmates, unsure whether they were being watched, would begin to act as if they were always under observation. This internalization of surveillance meant that the mere presence of a central watchtower—where the guard could potentially see everything—was enough to control the inmates' behavior.

The Panopticon works not through actual surveillance but through the *possibility* of being watched at any moment. This uncertainty is its most insidious feature. The prisoners, unable to distinguish when they are being observed from when they are not, begin to police themselves, moderating their own actions to avoid punishment. In time, this external control is internalized, transforming the prisoner's own mind into a surveillance mechanism.

In the 21st century, the Panopticon has evolved beyond the confines of a physical prison. It has become a metaphor for the pervasive systems of surveillance that govern modern life. Whether through governmental programs like COINTELPRO, which monitored political dissidents, or through the surveillance capitalism of today—where corporations mine personal data to predict and influence behavior—the Panopticon's shadow looms large over society.

COINTELPRO and the Mechanics of Surveillance

COINTELPRO, the FBI's covert Counter Intelligence Program, was a quintessential example of the Panopticon in action. Although not physically incarcerating activists, COINTELPRO subjected them to a form of psychological imprisonment. Through surveillance, disinformation, and infiltration, the FBI created an atmosphere in which targeted individuals and movements were constantly aware that they might be watched, monitored, or manipulated.

The activists of the Civil Rights Movement, the Black Panther Party, and other targeted groups lived in a state of uncertainty. They knew they were being observed but did not always know how or when. Wiretaps, informants, and government surveillance were pervasive, but the true extent of the FBI's operations remained shrouded in secrecy. This uncertainty fostered a climate of distrust, where activists were forced to question not only their surroundings but also their own actions and thoughts.

COINTELPRO's methods mirrored the Panopticon's psychological control. The activists, much like Bentham's prisoners, began to self-regulate, constantly aware that any misstep could result in consequences—be it arrest, discrediting, or worse. This constant monitoring eroded trust within movements, creating internal divisions and sapping the energy that could have been used to build solidarity and resist oppression.

The Modern Panopticon: Surveillance Capitalism and Data Mining

Today, the mechanisms of surveillance have expanded beyond government programs like COINTELPRO. We now live in what scholars refer to as a "surveillance capitalism" system, where personal data is the primary currency. Tech companies, social media platforms, and data brokers collect vast amounts of information about individuals—tracking their online behavior, preferences, locations, and even psychological profiles. This data is used to predict and influence behavior, shaping everything from consumer habits to political opinions.

Much like Bentham's Panopticon, this modern surveillance system works not because every individual is actively being watched at every moment, but because they *could be*. The knowledge that our actions—online and offline—are being tracked alters the way we behave. People may become more guarded in their communication, more careful about the information they share, and more susceptible to self-censorship, fearing the potential repercussions of their digital footprint.

Social media platforms, in particular, have blurred the line between voluntary and involuntary surveillance. Users willingly share vast amounts of personal information, often unaware of how it is being used or sold. Algorithms analyze this data to curate content, advertisements, and news that align with the user's preferences, creating echo chambers that reinforce existing beliefs. The result is a form of psychological manipulation that extends far beyond traditional surveillance, influencing not only how people act but how they think and perceive the world.

In this modern Panopticon, individuals become both the prisoners and the guards. We participate in our own surveillance, contributing to a system that commodifies our behavior, desires, and identities. The gaze of Big Brother is no longer a distant, omnipotent government entity—it is embedded in the very fabric of our digital lives.

The Psychological Effects of Living in the Panopticon

Living under constant or potential surveillance has profound psychological effects. Bentham's Panopticon was designed to make inmates internalize control, leading them to self-regulate even in the absence of direct observation. In the same way, modern surveillance systems—whether governmental or corporate—encourage individuals to internalize the gaze of the observer, modifying their behavior to avoid scrutiny or punishment.

Self-Censorship and Fear

One of the most immediate psychological effects of surveillance is self-censorship. When individuals believe they are being watched, they are less likely to engage in behaviors that could draw negative attention, even if those behaviors are not inherently harmful or illegal. This self-censorship can extend beyond actions to thoughts and ideas, as people begin to avoid expressing opinions or beliefs that might be perceived as controversial or subversive.

Under COINTELPRO, activists experienced this firsthand. Knowing they were under surveillance, many became more cautious in their speech and actions, fearing that any misstep could be used against them. The constant pressure of being watched led to anxiety, paranoia, and a sense of powerlessness. Activists were forced to question not only the loyalty of those around them but their own ability to resist the forces of control.

In the modern era, surveillance capitalism amplifies this effect. People are aware that their online behavior is being tracked—every click, search, and interaction is logged and analyzed. This awareness can lead to a form of digital self-censorship, where individuals are more guarded in what they share, post, or search for online. Fear of surveillance can stifle creativity, inhibit free expression, and create a culture of conformity, where people are hesitant to deviate from the norms established by the surveillance apparatus.

Paranoia and Distrust

The uncertainty of surveillance breeds paranoia. When individuals are unsure of when, how, or by whom they are being watched, they begin to see potential threats everywhere. This paranoia can lead to a breakdown in trust—not only in institutions but in personal relationships. Under COINTELPRO, the FBI deliberately sowed distrust within movements, planting informants and spreading disinformation

ZEN AND THE ART OF COINTELPRO

to create divisions. Activists were left wondering who among them might be an informant, undermining solidarity and weakening their collective resistance.

Today, the pervasive nature of surveillance has created a similar atmosphere of distrust. People are increasingly skeptical of the platforms they use, the companies that collect their data, and even the governments that claim to protect their privacy. This erosion of trust extends beyond the digital realm, affecting how individuals relate to each other in personal and professional settings. In a world where surveillance is ubiquitous, trust becomes a scarce and fragile commodity.

The Loss of Authenticity

Surveillance not only alters behavior but also impacts how individuals perceive themselves. When we are constantly aware of being watched, we may begin to perform for the observer, adopting behaviors, identities, or personas that conform to societal expectations. Over time, this performative aspect of surveillance can lead to a loss of authenticity, as individuals become disconnected from their true selves in favor of presenting a socially acceptable version of themselves.

This phenomenon was evident under COINTELPRO, where activists were forced to navigate the tension between their public and private selves. The knowledge that they were being watched influenced how they presented themselves to the world, often leading to a sense of fragmentation or alienation from their own identity. In the modern era, social media platforms exacerbate this effect, encouraging users to curate idealized versions of themselves that align with the expectations of their digital audience.

Zen and the Illusion of Surveillance

In Zen, one of the central teachings is that much of the suffering we experience arises from *illusion*—our attachments to things that are ultimately impermanent or unreal. Surveillance, in many ways, operates on a similar illusion: the idea that we are always being watched, that we must conform to external expectations, and that our behavior must be constantly modified to avoid scrutiny. This illusion traps us in a state of fear, self-censorship, and inauthenticity.

Zen practice offers a path toward waking up from this illusion. Through meditation, mindfulness, and the cultivation of awareness, we can begin to see through the constructs that govern our thoughts and behaviors. Surveillance, like many forms of control, is rooted in fear—fear of punishment, fear of judgment, and fear of the unknown. But Zen teaches us that fear itself is a construct of the mind, one that can be dissolved through practice.

Zazen: The Practice of Stillness and Awareness

Zazen, or seated meditation, is one of the core practices of Zen. In Zazen, the practitioner sits in stillness, observing the flow of thoughts, sensations, and emotions without attachment or judgment. This practice cultivates a state of *non-dual awareness*, where the distinction between observer and observed begins to dissolve. In this state, the mind is no longer trapped in the illusion of separation, and the fear of being watched loses its grip.

In the context of surveillance, Zazen can serve as a powerful antidote to the psychological effects of the Panopticon. When we sit in stillness, we confront the fear of being watched head-on. Rather than running from it or trying to control it, we allow it to be, without attachment or aversion. Over time, this practice helps to dissolve the illusion of surveillance, revealing that the only true observer is the mind itself.

Zazen also cultivates *authenticity*. In stillness, we come face to face with our true selves, unmediated by the expectations of others or the external gaze. This practice encourages us to live from a place of inner freedom, where our actions are not dictated by fear of surveillance but by a deep connection to our own values and intentions.

Mindfulness in the Age of Surveillance

Mindfulness, the practice of being fully present in the moment, offers another path toward reclaiming inner freedom in a surveillance society. When we are mindful, we are aware of our thoughts, actions, and surroundings without being dominated by them. This awareness creates a space of mental and emotional freedom, where we can choose how to respond to external pressures rather than being controlled by them.

In a world where surveillance is ubiquitous, mindfulness allows us to step out of the reactive patterns of fear and self-censorship. By cultivating a state of *non-reactive awareness*, we can observe the mechanisms of surveillance without being consumed by them. This practice helps us to maintain a sense of autonomy, even in the face of external control.

Waking Up in the Panopticon

To "wake up" in the Panopticon means to see through the illusion of surveillance and reclaim our inner freedom. Zen teaches that true freedom comes not from escaping external control but from transcending the internal mechanisms that bind us to fear and attachment. In the Panopticon, we are conditioned to believe that we are always being watched, that our actions are always subject to scrutiny, and that we must conform to avoid punishment. But this belief is an illusion, one that can be dissolved through awareness and practice.

By embracing Zen practices like Zazen and mindfulness, we can begin to wake up from the psychological grip of the Panopticon. We can see that the true prison is not the external gaze but the internalized fear that it creates. In this way, Zen offers a path toward liberation—a way to live authentically, mindfully, and freely, even in a world where surveillance is pervasive.

The Panopticon may shape the world around us, but it does not have to shape our inner lives. Through Zen practice, we can cultivate a state of awareness that transcends the fear of being watched, allowing us to live from a place of inner peace and authenticity. In this way, we can wake up in the Panopticon, reclaiming our freedom and our humanity in the process.

Breaking the Cycle of Oppression

The cycle of oppression—its mechanisms, structures, and psychology—has existed for as long as there have been power dynamics between individuals, groups, and states. COINTELPRO, the FBI's Counter Intelligence Program, represents one of the most insidious manifestations of this cycle in the modern age. Through surveillance, manipulation, and violence, the U.S. government sought to control, disrupt, and ultimately dismantle social and political movements that threatened the status quo. COINTELPRO was not an isolated incident but rather part of a broader historical pattern where power structures, feeling threatened by change, turn to oppressive tactics to maintain control.

But why does this cycle of oppression persist? Why do governments, institutions, and individuals resort to violence, fear, and manipulation when confronted with difference or dissent? The answer lies not only in the material realities of power and control but in the deeper spiritual dis-ease that afflicts individuals and societies alike. Zen Buddhism offers an alternative path—one rooted in non-attachment, compassion, and mindfulness—that can help break the cycle of oppression at both the individual and societal levels.

This chapter brings together Zen's teachings to explore how the principles of non-attachment, compassion, and awareness can be used as tools for healing and transformation. It suggests that societal control, manipulation, and violence are symptoms of deeper issues within the human mind and spirit, and that the process of breaking free from oppression must begin with the individual.

Oppression as a Symptom of Spiritual Dis-ease

Oppression is often understood as a material phenomenon—a system of control designed to maintain power, wealth, and privilege. While this is undoubtedly true, oppression also has a psychological and spiritual dimension that cannot be ignored. The urge to dominate, control, and exploit others is not simply a political or economic calculation but a reflection of deeper insecurities, fears, and attachments.

In Zen, suffering arises from attachment—attachment to the self, to desires, to outcomes, to identities, and to power. The more tightly we cling to these things, the more we experience fear, anxiety, and dissatisfaction. In the case of oppression, those in power are often driven by a deep-seated fear of losing control. They cling to their status, wealth, and authority, perceiving any challenge to the status quo as an existential threat.

COINTELPRO's operations were driven by this very fear. The social movements of the 1960s and 1970s—especially the Civil Rights Movement, the Black Panther Party, and the anti-war movements—represented a threat to the existing power structures in the United States. These movements sought to dismantle racial injustice, economic inequality, and imperialism, all of which were deeply embedded in the fabric of American society. Rather than engaging with these movements in a constructive way, the government responded with fear and repression, using COINTELPRO to undermine and destroy them from within.

This fear-based response reflects a profound spiritual dis-ease—a clinging to power, control, and identity that creates suffering not only for those who are oppressed but for the oppressors themselves. The architects of COINTELPRO were trapped in a cycle of fear and attachment, unable to see beyond their narrow understanding of security and stability. In their quest to preserve the status quo, they perpetuated a cycle of violence, manipulation, and control that continues to reverberate through society to this day.

Non-Attachment: Letting Go of the Need for Control

At the heart of Zen practice is the teaching of non-attachment. Non-attachment does not mean indifference or passivity; rather, it is the ability to engage with life fully without clinging to specific outcomes or identities. In the context of oppression, non-attachment offers a powerful tool for breaking the cycle of control and fear that drives oppressive systems.

Those who seek to oppress others are often deeply attached to their own power and status. They see the world in terms of hierarchies and divisions, clinging to the belief that their own security depends on maintaining control over others. This attachment leads to fear—fear of losing power, fear of change, fear of the unknown—and this fear, in turn, fuels the cycle of oppression.

Non-attachment offers a way out of this cycle. By letting go of the need for control, we can begin to dismantle the psychological structures that give rise to oppression. Non-attachment allows us to see that true security does not come from dominating others or maintaining rigid hierarchies but from a deeper connection to our own inner peace and wisdom.

In the context of COINTELPRO, the FBI's obsession with controlling and neutralizing social movements was a form of attachment—to the idea of a stable, unchanging social order. This attachment led to extreme measures, including illegal surveillance, infiltration, and the spread of disinformation. Yet, from a Zen perspective, this need for control was ultimately self-defeating. The more the government sought to suppress dissent, the more it created conditions of distrust, fear, and unrest—both within the targeted movements and within the broader society.

By practicing non-attachment, we can learn to let go of the fear-based need to control others and the world around us. This does not mean ignoring injustice or passively accepting oppression. Instead, it means recognizing that true change comes not from force or manipulation but from a deep commitment to ethical action and compassion. When we let go of the need to control others, we create space for healing, dialogue, and transformation.

Compassion: Extending Kindness to All Beings

Compassion is another core principle of Zen, and it is an essential element in breaking the cycle of oppression. Compassion involves recognizing the inherent dignity and worth of all beings, regardless of their actions or circumstances. It is the ability to see beyond the surface of human behavior and to understand the suffering that lies beneath.

In the context of COINTELPRO, extending compassion to those who were targeted by the government's surveillance and manipulation is relatively easy. The individuals and movements who fought for civil rights, equality, and justice were clearly on the side of righteousness, and their suffering was the result of an unjust and oppressive system.

But Zen challenges us to go further. It asks us to extend compassion not only to the victims of oppression but also to the oppressors themselves. This is a difficult and counterintuitive practice, particularly when we consider the actions of those responsible for COINTELPRO's operations—those who orchestrated illegal surveillance, spread disinformation, and used violence to undermine social justice movements.

Yet, from a Zen perspective, even the oppressors are deserving of compassion. Their actions, while harmful, are driven by their own suffering—their fear, attachment, and ignorance. By recognizing the humanity in those who oppress, we can begin to break the cycle of hatred and violence that perpetuates oppression. Compassion does not mean excusing or justifying harmful actions, but it does mean understanding that all beings, even those who do harm, are caught in the web of suffering.

The practice of compassion invites us to see beyond the duality of victim and oppressor. In the interconnected web of existence, both the oppressed and the oppressor are bound together in a cycle of suffering. The oppressor, through their actions, creates suffering not only for those they oppress but for themselves. Their attachment to power, control, and identity creates a prison of fear and anxiety from which they cannot escape. By extending compassion to the oppressor, we acknowledge their suffering and open the door to healing and transformation.

Compassion also requires that we extend kindness to ourselves. In the face of oppression, it is easy to become consumed by anger, hatred, and resentment. These emotions, while understandable, can trap us in the very cycle we seek to break. Zen teaches that true liberation comes not from feeding the flames of anger but from cultivating inner peace and clarity. By practicing compassion for ourselves, we can move beyond the reactive patterns of fear and anger and act from a place of wisdom and strength.

Mindfulness: Awakening to the Present Moment

Mindfulness, the practice of being fully present in the moment, is another key tool for breaking the cycle of oppression. Oppressive systems thrive on fear, confusion, and distraction. They seek to keep individuals and societies trapped in reactive patterns of thought and behavior, unable to see clearly or act with intention.

ZEN AND THE ART OF COINTELPRO

Mindfulness offers a way to cut through the noise of oppression and connect with the present moment. By cultivating awareness of our thoughts, emotions, and surroundings, we can begin to see through the illusions that keep us bound to cycles of fear and attachment. Mindfulness allows us to step back from the reactive mind and respond to oppression with clarity and intention.

In the context of COINTELPRO, mindfulness can help us understand the psychological impact of surveillance and manipulation. The FBI's tactics were designed to create confusion, mistrust, and paranoia within social movements. Activists were forced to question the loyalty of their comrades, to second-guess their own decisions, and to live in a state of constant fear. This psychological warfare was as damaging as the physical repression, undermining the mental and emotional well-being of those targeted.

Mindfulness provides a way to resist this psychological manipulation. By staying present and aware, we can see through the tactics of fear and confusion and maintain our sense of inner peace and autonomy. Mindfulness also helps us to stay grounded in our values and intentions, even in the face of external pressure. When we are mindful, we are less likely to be swayed by fear or manipulation, and more likely to act with clarity and purpose.

Breaking the Cycle: Healing Through Ethical Action and Peace

STEVE SHORT

Zen teaches that true transformation begins within. If we wish to break the cycle of oppression, we must first address the spiritual and psychological roots of oppression within ourselves. This means cultivating non-attachment, compassion, and mindfulness in our own lives and using these tools to engage with the world in a way that promotes healing and peace.

But inner transformation is not enough. Breaking the cycle of oppression also requires *ethical action*. Zen emphasizes the importance of right action—actions that are in alignment with our deepest values and that promote the well-being of all beings. In the face of oppression, this means standing up for justice, equality, and dignity, while also acting from a place of compassion and wisdom.

Ethical action is not about defeating or destroying the oppressor but about creating the conditions for healing and transformation. This means addressing the systemic causes of oppression, such as inequality, racism, and economic exploitation, while also recognizing the shared humanity of all beings. By acting with integrity and compassion, we can begin to dismantle the structures of oppression and create a society based on justice, peace, and mutual respect.

Finally, breaking the cycle of oppression requires *the cultivation of peace within*. Zen teaches that peace is not something that can be imposed from the outside but must be cultivated from within. When we are at peace with ourselves—when we are free from fear, attachment, and delusion—we create the conditions for peace in the world around us. Peace is not

ZEN AND THE ART OF COINTELPRO

passive; it is an active process of engaging with the world from a place of clarity, compassion, and non-attachment.

The cycle of oppression that COINTELPRO represents is not just a political or social phenomenon but a reflection of deeper spiritual dis-ease. By embracing the teachings of Zen—non-attachment, compassion, and mindfulness—we can begin to heal the wounds of oppression and create a path forward toward a more just and peaceful world. Breaking the cycle of oppression requires both inner transformation and ethical action, as we work to dismantle the systems of control and violence that perpetuate suffering while cultivating peace and healing within ourselves and in the world.

The Zen of Freedom

In a world rife with control, surveillance, and manipulation, the concept of freedom often feels elusive. We live in a time when our movements are tracked, our communications monitored, and our choices influenced by unseen forces. COINTELPRO, the FBI's notorious Counter Intelligence Program, serves as a stark reminder of how power structures can undermine the very freedoms they claim to protect. Yet, the most profound lesson from the history of COINTELPRO and the social movements it sought to dismantle is that true freedom transcends the physical and political. It resides not in the absence of external control, but in the inner liberation from the mind's attachments, fears, and delusions. This is the Zen of freedom, and it is the freedom that no surveillance state or oppressive system can take away.

In this final chapter, we explore the Zen philosophy of freedom—how liberation begins within the individual, how it relates to the collective struggle for justice, and how both personal enlightenment and social transformation are deeply intertwined. Drawing on the resilience of those who resisted COINTELPRO's tactics and the enduring teachings of Zen, this chapter closes with a vision of freedom that is not only achievable but essential for personal and societal healing.

External Freedom vs. Inner Freedom

Throughout history, individuals and movements have fought for external freedom—freedom from tyranny, from

ZEN AND THE ART OF COINTELPRO

oppression, from systems of control that stifle human potential. The fight for civil rights, gender equality, and economic justice are all manifestations of this drive for liberation. Yet, Zen challenges us to look beyond the external circumstances and consider a more fundamental kind of freedom: the inner freedom from the mind's own limitations.

External freedom, as crucial as it is, is always subject to change. Governments rise and fall, laws shift, and societies evolve. But inner freedom—the freedom to be at peace with oneself, to transcend the ego's constant craving for security and control—remains within our reach no matter the external conditions. This is the kind of freedom that Zen teaches, and it is the freedom that those targeted by COINTELPRO were able to cultivate in the face of intense repression.

Consider the activists, revolutionaries, and ordinary citizens who were subjected to COINTELPRO's tactics. Many were under constant surveillance, their homes infiltrated, their relationships sabotaged by government operatives. The psychological toll of living under such scrutiny, of having one's every move watched and manipulated, was immense. And yet, many of these individuals found ways to resist not only through protests and organizing but through cultivating an inner strength that could not be broken.

Zen teaches that the mind's attachment to external conditions—whether it be the desire for safety, recognition, or even freedom itself—creates suffering. We see this in COINTELPRO's own downfall. The FBI's obsessive need to control, to neutralize what it saw as threats to the social order, became a form of self-sabotage. In its quest to maintain order, the government created chaos, not only in the movements it targeted but within its own ranks. Fear, suspicion, and mistrust spread through both the oppressed and the oppressors, leading to a spiral of paranoia that ultimately undermined the FBI's goals.

The paradox of control is that the more we cling to it, the more we lose it. Zen offers a way out of this paradox by teaching that true freedom comes not from controlling the external world but from letting go of the need to control it. This does not mean passivity or resignation. Rather, it means cultivating the kind of inner liberation that allows us to engage with the world from a place of clarity, compassion, and resilience.

The Illusion of Security

At the heart of COINTELPRO's operations was a fear-driven desire for security. The social movements of the 1960s and 1970s—especially the Civil Rights Movement, the Black Power Movement, and the anti-war protests—represented a perceived threat to the stability of the U.S. government and its existing power structures. In response, the FBI sought to neutralize these movements through surveillance, infiltration, and disinformation. But what COINTELPRO ultimately revealed was not the power of the state but its deep insecurity.

Zen teaches that security, like control, is an illusion. The world is in a constant state of flux, and no amount of surveillance or repression can create permanent stability. The FBI's attempts to control social change through COINTELPRO were

ZEN AND THE ART OF COINTELPRO

ultimately futile because they were based on a false premise: that security could be achieved by stifling dissent and maintaining the status quo. In reality, the only constant is change, and true freedom lies in accepting this impermanence rather than trying to resist it.

In Zen, the practice of non-attachment is a way to break free from the mind's obsessive need for security. Non-attachment does not mean detachment or indifference, but rather a deep acceptance of life as it is, without clinging to specific outcomes. This kind of inner freedom allows individuals to face uncertainty and change without being paralyzed by fear.

For the activists targeted by COINTELPRO, cultivating this kind of non-attachment was essential to their survival. They had to navigate a world in which their movements were being constantly monitored, their leaders discredited, and their efforts to create change undermined at every turn. But those who were able to let go of the need for external validation, who could continue their work even in the face of betrayal and manipulation, found a deeper kind of freedom—one that COINTELPRO could never take away.

Freedom from Fear

Fear was one of COINTELPRO's most powerful weapons. By spreading disinformation, sowing discord, and infiltrating movements, the FBI sought to create an atmosphere of paranoia and mistrust. Fear is a powerful tool of control because it narrows our vision, making us more likely to act out of desperation or self-preservation rather than wisdom or compassion.

Zen teaches that fear is a product of the mind's attachment to self and to outcomes. We fear what we cannot control, and the more we try to control the world around us, the more fearful we become. The way to break free from fear is not to eliminate threats or to create perfect security but to cultivate a mind that is free from attachment.

In the context of COINTELPRO, fear was both the means and the end of oppression. The FBI's tactics were designed to instill fear in activists, to make them question their comrades, their purpose, and even their own worth. But fear also consumed the oppressors themselves. The government's fear of social change, of losing control, led it to engage in increasingly desperate and illegal tactics, ultimately undermining its own legitimacy.

The Zen of freedom teaches us that fear can be transcended through mindfulness and compassion. By bringing awareness to the present moment, we can see fear for what it is—a mental construct, a projection of the mind's insecurities. When we are fully present, fear loses its power over us. We can act not out of fear but out of wisdom and love.

For those who lived under the constant threat of COINTELPRO, mindfulness became a form of resistance. By staying grounded in the present moment, they were able to see through the FBI's tactics of manipulation and fear. They understood that the true battle was not just against an external oppressor but against the internal forces of fear, doubt, and division. By cultivating inner freedom, they were able to continue their work for justice with clarity and resilience, even in the face of overwhelming odds.

Collective Liberation: The Interconnectedness of Personal and Social Freedom

One of the most profound lessons of Zen is the teaching of interconnectedness—what Buddhists refer to as *interbeing*. In Zen, the self is not a separate, isolated entity but is deeply connected to all other beings and the world around it. This understanding of interconnectedness has profound implications for both personal and social freedom.

COINTELPRO sought to destroy movements by turning individuals against each other, by fostering division and mistrust. This strategy relied on the illusion of separateness—the idea that individuals could be isolated, manipulated, and pitted against one another. But those who resisted COINTELPRO understood that their liberation was bound up with the liberation of others. They recognized that their strength lay in solidarity, in the collective struggle for justice and equality.

Zen teaches that personal enlightenment and collective liberation are not separate goals but are deeply intertwined. True freedom cannot be achieved in isolation from others. The liberation of one person contributes to the liberation of all, and the liberation of society creates the conditions for individual freedom.

The movements targeted by COINTELPRO understood this principle intuitively. Whether it was the Civil Rights Movement's call for racial justice, the Black Panther Party's demand for economic equality, or the anti-war movement's opposition to imperialism, these movements were not just fighting for the rights of a particular group but for the liberation of all people from systems of oppression and violence.

Zen calls us to see beyond the dualities of self and other, victim and oppressor, and to recognize the interconnectedness of all beings. When we understand this interconnectedness, we realize that our own freedom is bound up with the freedom of others. We cannot be truly free as long as others are oppressed, and we cannot work for social justice without cultivating inner peace and clarity.

Mindful, Compassionate Action: The Path to True Freedom

The final lesson of Zen is that freedom is not a passive state but an active process. It is something we must cultivate through mindful, compassionate action. Zen teaches that enlightenment is not an abstract goal but a way of being in the world—a way of engaging with life that is rooted in awareness, compassion, and non-attachment.

For those who seek to break free from the cycles of oppression, this means that both personal and social liberation require ongoing practice. Mindfulness helps us stay present and clear, allowing us to see through the illusions that keep us trapped in fear, attachment, and division. Compassion guides us to act in ways that promote the well-being of all beings, rather than perpetuating systems of harm.

COINTELPRO was designed to destroy movements, to divide and conquer. But those who resisted its tactics did so not just through external actions but through a deep commitment to their values and principles. They understood that true freedom could not be taken away by external forces as long as they remained rooted in their inner freedom.

The Zen of freedom teaches us that liberation is not something we can achieve once and for all, but something we must continually cultivate. It requires us to engage with the world mindfully, to act with compassion and integrity, and to remain unattached to specific outcomes. In doing so, we create the conditions for both personal enlightenment and social justice.

The Zen of Freedom in a World of Control

As we close this exploration of COINTELPRO and Zen philosophy, we return to the central theme: true freedom transcends external circumstances. Whether we live in a surveillance state or a society of relative freedom, the path to liberation lies within. It is the freedom from fear, from attachment, from the mind's delusions.

But this inner freedom is not disconnected from the world. As Zen teaches, personal enlightenment and social justice are deeply intertwined. The work of liberation is both internal and external, and by cultivating mindfulness, compassion, and non-attachment, we can contribute to the healing of ourselves and society.

The legacy of COINTELPRO is a reminder of the dangers of control and fear, but it is also a testament to the resilience of those who fought for freedom. In the face of oppression, they showed us that true freedom comes not from overthrowing external systems but from liberating the mind and acting with integrity in the world.

This is the Zen of freedom, and it is a path that is open to all of us. Through mindful, compassionate action, we can break free from the cycles of control and fear, and create a world that reflects the deeper truths of justice, peace, and interconnectedness.

Don't miss out!

Visit the website below and you can sign up to receive emails whenever Steve Short publishes a new book. There's no charge and no obligation.

https://books2read.com/r/B-A-RGJNC-PIRBF

BOOKS 2 READ

Connecting independent readers to independent writers.

About the Author

Steve Short is a writer, historian, and lifelong student of Eastern philosophy, with a particular focus on Zen Buddhism. Drawing from his diverse experiences in political activism and meditation practice, Steve explores the intersection of government power, societal control, and personal liberation in his writing. He is dedicated to helping readers find clarity and freedom in an increasingly complex and surveillance-driven world.

Milton Keynes UK
Ingram Content Group UK Ltd.
UKHW020049181024
449757UK00011B/577